专业与卓越

2015年上海教师教学国际调查结果概要

教师教学国际调查中国上海项目组

上海教育出版社
SHANGHAI EDUCATIONAL
PUBLISHING HOUSE

ZHUANYE

YU

ZHUOYUE

TALIS国际机构：
经济合作与发展组织(OECD，法国巴黎)

TALIS国际协作机构：
国际教育成就评价协会（IEA，荷兰阿姆斯特丹）
国际教育评价协会数据处理与研究中心（IEA DPC，德国汉堡）
加拿大统计局（Statistics Canada, 加拿大渥太华）
澳大利亚教育研究院（ACER, 澳大利亚墨尔本）

上海项目组织机构：
上海市教育委员会TALIS项目领导小组
上海师范大学国际与比较教育研究院
上海TALIS秘书处/研究中心

联系我们：
上海师范大学国际与比较教育研究院
上海TALIS秘书处/研究中心
电话：021-64321077
电邮：talis_shanghai98@vip.163.com
地址：上海市桂林路100号上海师范大学教苑楼1102室

目　录

调查了这些国家（地区）初中教师和校长，并于 2009 年发布了第一份报告——《营造有效的教与学环境：TALIS 首次调查结果》。

2013 年至 2014 年，新一轮的 TALIS 在全世界 34 个国家（地区）开展。同年，OECD 为包括上海在内的 4 个新参与国家（地区）开展了 TALIS 2013+ 调查。除了调查进行时间的差异（2015年上半年完成），TALIS 2013+ 调查内容与技术标准与 2013 年的 TALIS 调查完全相同。因此，38 个参与国家（地区）的 11 万余教师、校长的问卷调查数据具有可比性[1]。

教师教学国际调查（TALIS）项目主要是通过对学校校长和教师的问卷调查来进行的。问卷由经合组织委托专业机构设计，经参与国理事会批准实施。按照经合组织统一的规定，所有参与国（地区）都应有 200 所初中、每所初中有 20 位教师和 1 位校长参与问卷调查。经合组织用统一的技术标准、统一的运作工具抽取各国参与学校和各学校中参与调查的教师样本。目前，TALIS 已经扩大到高中和小学学段的教师调查。除了必须参与初中学段教师的调查，各国可以自行决定是否参加其他学段的教师调查。

TALIS 调查包括教师问卷和校长问卷两个部分（表 1）。其中教师问卷 52 道题目，含 7 大主题，分别为背景信息、教师专业发展、教师反馈、教学概况、教学、学校氛围和工作满意度以及出国培训情况；校长问卷共计 41 道题目，包含 8 个调查主题，分别为

---

[1] 本书使用了 36 个国家（地区）的数据进行分析，冰岛和美国的数据没有包含在计算中。冰岛的数据没有获得，美国的数据没有达到 TALIS 技术标准。

个人背景信息、专业发展、学校背景信息、学校领导力、教师正式评价、学校风气、教师入职与带教和工作满意度情况。除了各有大量的独特内容，教师与校长的问卷中，还有相互印证的内容。

为更好地了解各国（地区）的情况，经合组织允许各国（地区）在教师和校长问卷调查中增加若干自选问题。上海根据本地的情况，在教师问卷中增加了3道上海教师的专业发展的题目，在校长问卷中增加了2道背景信息题目。

表1　TALIS 2013+ 上海问卷调查主题和题目分析

	调查主题	题目量	主要内容
教师问卷	教师个人背景信息	18（1-18）	性别、年龄、教龄，就业性质，班级情况，职前教育，工作时间
	教师专业发展	12（19-30，51-52）	入职培训类型，专业发展活动类型、时间、主题分布、影响，专业发展支持、方式、需求、阻碍因素。教研活动频率、主要内容和形式、科研活动评价。教师出国培训
	教师评价反馈	4（31-34）	反馈来源、反馈内容、反馈作用、反馈感受
	教学概况	3（35-37）	教学观、教学合作、教学能力
	特定班级的教学	9（38-46）	班级构成、教授科目、班额、课堂时间分配、纪律、教学策略、评估方式

（续表）

	调查主题	题目量	主要内容
教师问卷	学校风气和工作满意度	4（47-50）	决策参与、学生重视、工作满意度、个人特质
校长问卷	个人背景信息	7（1-7）	性别、年龄、工作经验、教育水平、专业准备等
	校长专业发展	3（8-10）	专业发展活动（参与度、强度）、阻碍专业发展活动的因素
	学校背景信息	7（11-17）	所处区域、公办/民办、学校竞争性、学生规模、个别学生群体所占比例、学校资源状况
	校长领导力状况	10（18-28）	校长工作时间分布、教学领导力状况、工作障碍等
	教师的正式评价	3（29-31）	评价主体、频率、评价反馈
	学校风气	3（32-34）	学校氛围、师生关系、影响教学能力的因素、纪律风气
	教师入职与带教	6（35-40）	新教师入职培训、入职培训的形式、带教机会、校长对带教重要性的认识
	工作满意度	1（41）	校长对工作环境的满意度，校长对职业的满意度

二、上海参加 TALIS 的原因

除了家庭，学校是学生发展最重要的场所，而在所有的学校因素中，教师无疑是最为重要的因素。上海学生在 PISA 2009 和 PISA 2012 三个主要学科领域的优异表现无疑与上海的教师队伍有非常紧密的关系。尽管上海 PISA 2012 和 TALIS 2013+ 的样本并不一致，调查时间差异也比较大，但两者的结果均反映了上海基础教育整体的状况。因此我们可以通过国际比较大致了解上海教师队伍对学生学习的影响。

在 PISA 所引发的对上海教育的全球性讨论热潮中，国内外研究者不约而同地将目光聚焦到上海教师的身上。上海如何选拔教师，如何培养教师？上海教师如何工作、如何学习、如何发展都成为世界各国来访者们关心的话题。经合组织的 TALIS 项目为我们提供了一个很好的机会，通过 TALIS，我们可以在国际平台上深入了解上海教师队伍建设自身的特征，总结我们在教师队伍建设方面的成功经验。另一方面，上海基础教育在取得巨大成就的同时，仍存在一些缺失和不足，问题的解决有赖于从教师和教学方面入手去寻找原因和改变方法。在这方面，TALIS 也能为我们提供很好的启发和借鉴。这些内容不仅对上海编制十三五教育规划提供坚实的证据，更能不断促进上海教育决策的科学化发展。

最后，参与国际性的教师调查项目有利于我们深入了解和学习当前教师研究领域的方法、技术和经验，这反过来将会很大程度上促进上海建立自己的多元教师评价体系。

三、 上海 TALIS 项目架构

上海市教委在 2014 年 4 月决定参加 TALIS 2013+ 调查。该项目由教委王平副主任直接领导并负责,上海师范大学国际与比较教育研究院张民选院长为国家(地区)项目负责人,秘书处和研究中心设在上海师范大学国际与比较教育研究院。

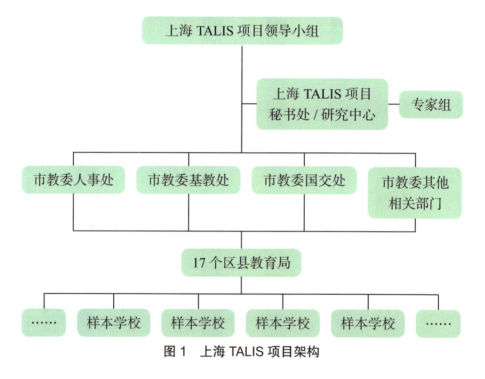

图 1 上海 TALIS 项目架构

TALIS 项目的开展,需要包括人事处、基教处、国交处在内的上海市教委多个相关部门的协调,涵盖全市 17 个区县教育局在内的职能部门的支持配合,最终才能在各样本学校顺利开展。

四、上海 TALIS 2013+ 测试样本及参与率

上海初中教师的样本是严格按照 TALIS 相关的技术规范进行抽样获得的。TALIS 采用两阶段分层抽样。第一阶段是学校抽样，采用与规模成比例的等概率抽样方式，上海按照学校办学体制和所处位置两个外显变量对学校进行分类。第二阶段是学校内教师抽样，采用完全随机抽样方式进行。

2015 年 1 月 9 日，上海全市 199 所初中学校（初中，以及九年一贯制学校和完中初中部分）共 3925 名初中教师参加了 TALIS 2013+ 调查，他们可以代表全市 36628 位初中教师。同时，教师所在学校校长共 193 名完成了校长问卷。

表 2　上海教师样本和代表性

外显类别	样本学校数	无法参加的样本学校	参加的样本学校	参加测试的教师数量	参加测试的校长数
公办－市区	70	1	69	1333	68
公办－郊区	90	0	90	1795	87
民办－市区	16	0	16	320	15
民办－郊区	24	0	24	477	23
小计	200	1	199	3925	193

加权后，上海 TALIS 2013+ 的学校参与率为 100%，教师参与率达 99.0%，总体参与率为 99.0%，样本具有很好的代表性。

第二部分：上海 TALIS 的教师调查结果

一、上海初中教师概况

1. 教师的年龄与教龄分布

上海初中教师的平均年龄为 38 岁，比国际均值低 5 岁，是所有参加 TALIS 的国家（地区）中除新加坡外最年轻的群体。分年龄段来看，上海教师主要集中在 30 至 39 岁和 40 至 49 岁两个年龄段，两段合并的比例达 73.0%。30 岁以下的年轻教师占总体的 17.9%，50 岁以上至 60 岁的教师比例相对较少，占 9.1%。

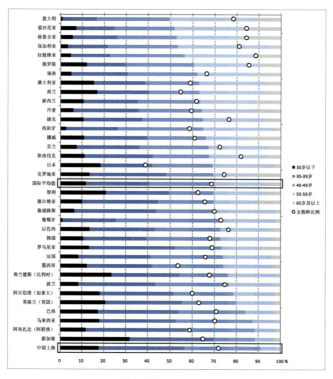

图 2　教师的年龄和性别分布

　　然而，尽管上海初中教师群体非常年轻，但教师的平均任教年数并不短，平均达 15.5 年，仅比 TALIS 国际均值 16.5 年少 1 年。在所有国家（地区）中，新加坡的教师平均年龄最小，比上海平均小约 2 岁，但其任教年数也是最少的，仅为 9.7 年。

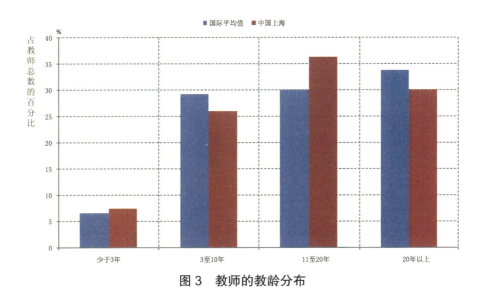

图 3　教师的教龄分布

　　可以看到，上海教师中，工作经验在 11 至 20 年的比例最大，占 36.3%，其次是 10 年以内的占 33.5%，20 年以上教龄的教师占 30.1%。TALIS 国家平均而言，10 年内教龄的教师最多，占 36.0%，其次是 20 年以上教龄的，占 33.9%，中间段教师最少，占 30.1%。在所有国家（地区）中，新加坡 3 年内教龄的教师最多，占总数的 20.4%，10 年内教龄的教师占到总数的 68.2%，可见，新加坡的教师群体是非常年轻的队伍。

2. 教师的性别分布

如图 2 所示，除日本外，所有 TALIS 国家（地区）均为女性教师占多数，国际平均而言，女教师的比例达 68.8%。在上海，初中女教师比例显著高于国际均值，达 72.2%。这表明，在绝大多数国家（地区），女性仍是初中教师群体的主要来源。

有意思的是，尽管绝大多数国家女性教师比例远高于男性教师，但在几乎所有 TALIS 参与国家（地区）中，相对教师中女性所占的比例，校长中女性所占比例明显偏低。

二、教师的职前教育和入职培训

1. 教师的学历水平分布

在上海，接受过大学本科及以上水平教育的初中教师占 98.5%，其中，大学本科学历的教师占 89.4%，研究生学历（含硕士和博士）教师占 9.1%，上海初中教师学历处于较高的水平。绝大多数国家的初中教师均受过大学本科及以上的教育，TALIS 国际均值为 91.2%。新加坡教师本科及以上的比例略高于国际平均值，为 92.7%。

相对而言，在一些国家（地区），例如葡萄牙、捷克、西班牙，初中教师中博士研究生的比例也比较高。上海初中阶段的教师中，博士学历的仅为 0.05%。

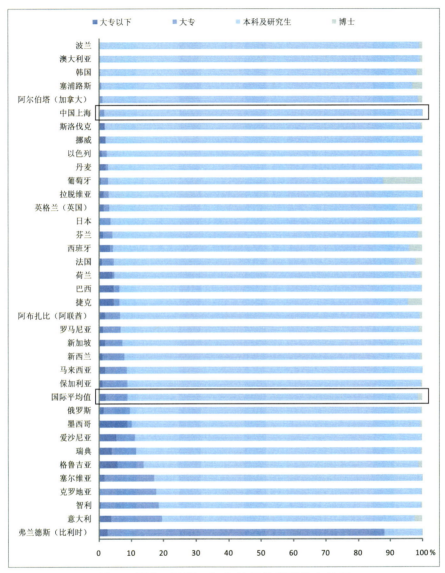

图4　国家（地区）初中教师的学历分布情况

2. 教师接受的师范专业训练

TALIS 将教师接受师范教育和教师培训视为教师接受的专业训练。在这方面，上海教师处于较高水平，教师中完成教师教育

11

或教师培训项目的比例占总体的98.2%，与新加坡（99.1%）处于同一水平。相对而言，国际平均比例仅为90.4%。

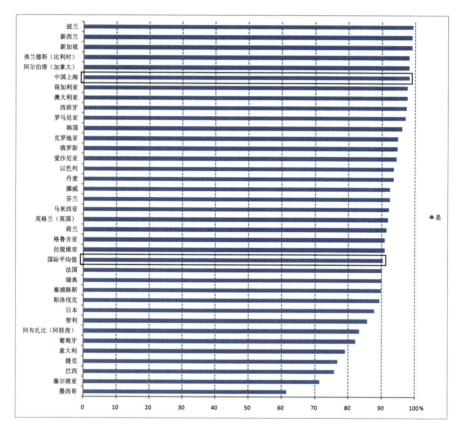

图5 国家（地区）初中教师接受师范教育和教师培训的情况

上海教师报告所接受的师范教育或教师培训内容是比较完善的。仅1.2%的教师认为教育或培训中没有包含所教科目的学科内容，2.1%的上海教师认为没有包含所教科目的教学法，4.9%的教师认为没有包含所教科目的课堂实践（如实习、见习或试教）。新加坡教师在学科内容上训练不如上海，认为没有包括教师的占2.8%，但课堂实践上训练比上海更多，认为没有包括的仅为1.6%，在教育教学方法方面（新加坡 1.8%），两者不存在显著差异。

3. 教师专业准备的自信程度

教师的专业准备反映的是教师对教学内容、教育教学方法和课堂实践的自信程度。

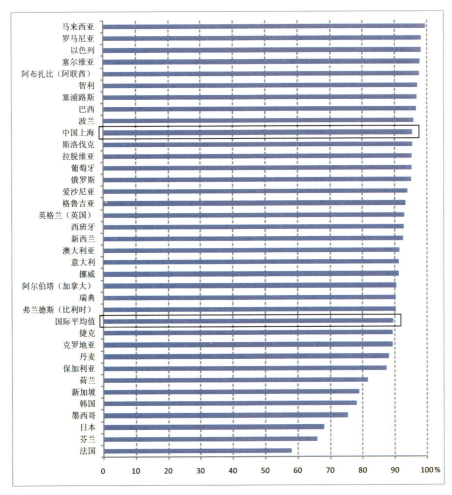

图 6　国家（地区）教师对所教学科内容的准备充分程度

　　在所教科目学科内容上，上海教师认为自己准备比较充分和非常充分的占 97.9%，相应的国际均值为 93.9%。上海教师对学科内容的自信程度显著优于国际均值。

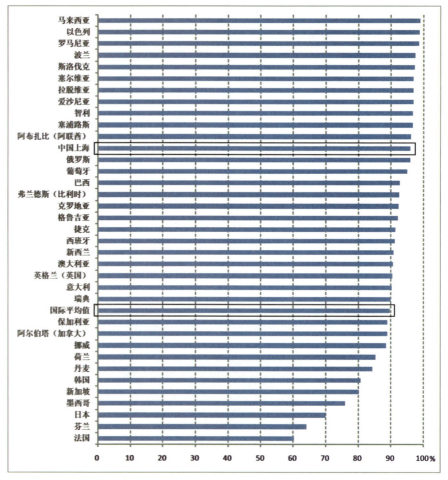

图 7　国家（地区）教师对所教学科教学法的准备充分程度

　　在所教科目学科教学法方面，上海教师认为自己准备比较充分和非常充分的占 96.0%，相应的国际均值为 89.7%。上海教师对教学方法的自信程度显著优于国际均值。

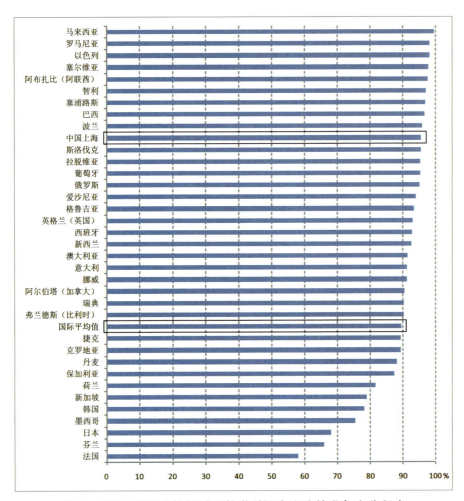

图8　国家（地区）教师对所教学科课堂实践的准备充分程度

　　在所教学科的课堂实践方面，上海教师认为自己准备比较充分和非常充分的占 95.4%。相应的国际均值为 89.5%。上海教师对课堂实践的自信程度同样显著优于国际均值。

　　综合来看，在衡量教师对所教学科教学准备充分程度的三个方面，绝大部分教师均做出积极的回应。这从一个侧面反映了上海教师在专业方面的自信程度。

4. 新教师参与正式入职培训的情况

上海几乎所有学校（99.2%）都向教师提供正式入职培训，同时，接近9成（89.0%）的教师报告参与正式的入职培训。新加坡（100%）、英格兰（99.4%）的学校也几乎都向教师提供正式入职培训，但教师报告参加的比例却明显低于上海，分别是80.0%和75.8%。

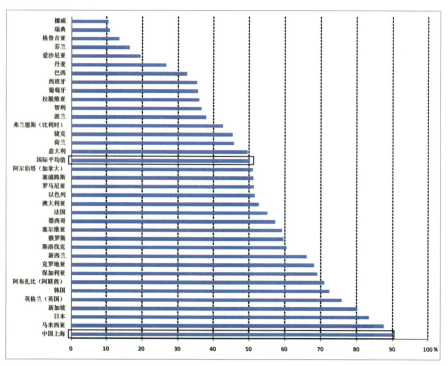

图9　各国（地区）教师报告参与正式入职培训的比例

对于3年以内的上海新教师而言，其所在学校提供正式入职培训的占99.7%，教师参与正式入职培训的达97.4%。新加坡的学校新教师所在学校提供正式入职培训的占 100%，新教师参与的达 96.9%。

5. 教师间的带教活动

上海所有学校（100%）都向教师提供带教活动。相应的国际均值仅为 70%，而在英格兰和新加坡，几乎所有学校也提供带教活动。

在上海，所有初中学校（100%）校长报告，大多数时候带教教师的主要学科领域与被带教教师的完全一致，国际均值为 69.5%，新加坡为 85.5%。

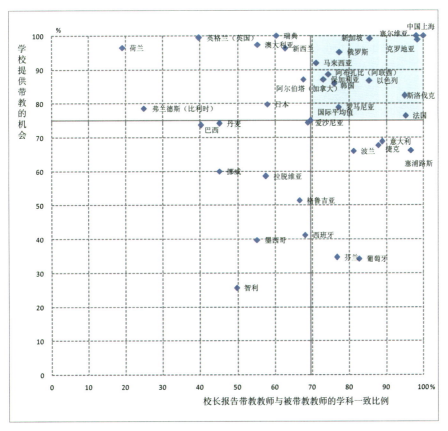

图 10　各国（地区）学校提供的带教机会与带教教师的学科一致性

上海教师参加带教活动的比例远高于国际平均值。报告目前有带教老师的教师占 23.0%，而报告目前作为带教老师的教师占 29.8%。相应的国际均值为 13.2% 和 14.9%。在新加坡，被带教（39.6%）和承担带教（39.4%）的教师比例更高，这可能与新加坡年轻教师居多有关系。

三、教师专业发展活动特征

1. 专业发展活动的参与率高

上海初中教师在过去一年参加过某种形式的专业发展活动

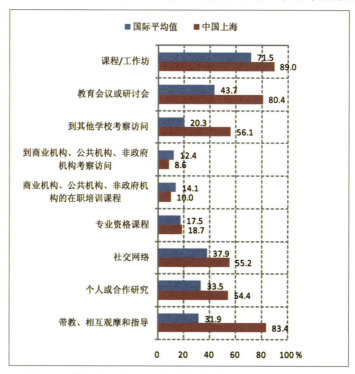

图 11　教师在过去一年参与各类专业发展活动的比例

的比例占总体的 97.7%，与新加坡（98.0%）和加拿大阿尔伯塔（97.7%）同属参与率最高的国家（地区）。国际平均而言，教师专业发展参与率仅为 88.7%。

上海教师参加较多的活动有"课程／工作坊""带教、相互观摩和指导""教育会议或研讨会"，均在 80% 以上，参与教师比例均高于国际平均水平。

2. 专业发展强度大

上海教师一年中用于各项专业发展活动的天数达 62.8 天（三

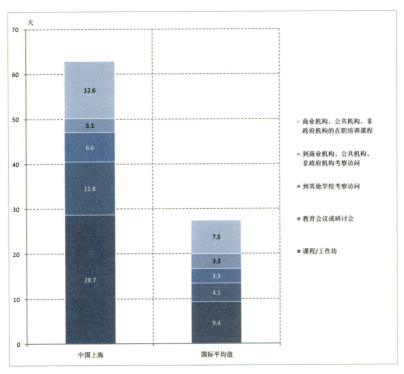

图 12　教师在过去一年参与各类专业发展活动的持续天数

个月的工作日时间)。相应的国际均值不及上海的一半, 仅为 27.6 天。天数较长的国家 (地区) 还有巴西 (68.8) 和格鲁吉亚 (61.3) 均超过 60 天, 持续时间最短的国家有比利时弗兰德斯、挪威、英格兰、瑞典和芬兰, 均低于 14 天。新加坡的时间仅为 21.6 天。

具体来说, 上海教师在课程 / 工作坊上平均花费 28.7 天, 参加商业机构、公共机构、非政府机构的在职培训课程的时间为 12.6 天, 在教育会议或研讨会方面平均花费 11.8 天, 三项时间均远高于国际平均值。

3. 参与课程与教学培训的活动最多

上海教师近一年参加的专业发展活动中,"所教学科领域的知

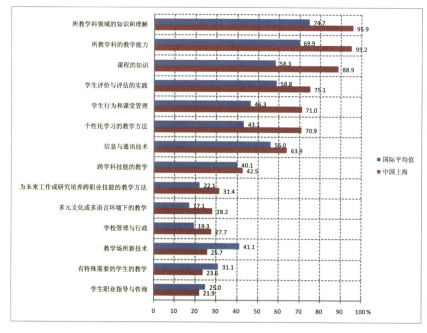

图 13　教师参与的专业发展活动主题分布情况

识和理解"（95.9%）、"所教学科的教学能力"(95.2%)、"课程的知识"(88.9%) 三个主题被专业发展活动涵盖的比例都非常高，远高于国际均值 74.7%，69.9% 和 58.3%。新加坡教师参与这三个主题的比例均低于上海 8-10 个百分点。

4. 重视个性化学习的教学方法

有 70.9% 的上海教师报告过去一年参与了个性化教学方法的专业发展活动，是所有国家中比例最高的。同时，在所有教师需要的专业发展活动中，上海教师选择个性化学习教学方法的最多，达 75.1%。在这方面，新加坡的教师与上海教师很不相同，参与该项专业发展的教师仅占 39.1%，低于国际平均值 43.1%。而教师对个性化学习的教学方法的需求也显著低于上海，仅为 57.8%。

但在其他多样化和差异化专业发展内容上，上海教师参与的比例介于 20% 至 45% 之间，都不太高。尽管如此，在多元文化和语言下教学（28.2%）、跨学科技能的教学（42.5%）、为未来工作或研究培养跨职业技能的教学（31.4%）以及学校管理与行政（27.7%）方面，上海教师的参与比例仍超过了 TALIS 国际均值。

值得注意的是，上海教师参与最少的专业发展活动是"学生职业指导"（21.9%）、"有特殊需要学生的教学"（23.6%）、"教学场所新技术"（25.7%）。这三项的参与率分别比国际均值低 15.4、7.5 和 3.0 个百分点（国际均值分别为 25.00%、31.1% 和 41.1%）。并且，上海教师需要教学场所新技术和有特殊需要学生教学方面专业发展的比例也明显低于国际平均水平。

5. 从时间和激励措施方面支持教师专业发展

分析表明，获得固定时间支持更多的国家（地区），相应的教师参加专业发展活动的比例一般也更高。上海认为有固定时间参加工作时间内专业发展活动的教师占 87.8%，和马来西亚（88.0%）同属比例最高的两个国家（地区），新加坡相应的比例仅为 70.3%，国际平均水平仅 54.9%。

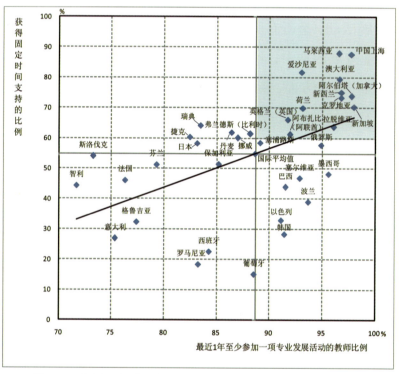

图 14 获得固定时间支持与教师参与专业发展活动的关系

但在专业发展活动的费用支持方面，新加坡有 89.7% 的教师无须付费，仅次于英格兰的 92.7%。相对而言，上海教师也有 80.4% 的教师报告无须承担专业发展费用，但该比例低于支持力度更大的英格兰、新加坡等 10 个国家和地区。

对上海教师而言，与工作时间冲突（58.6%）、缺少激励措施（51.6%）和与家庭责任时间冲突（40.3%）仍是参加专业发展活动最主要的障碍。

四、教师的教学特征

1. 认同建构主义教学理念

上海教师普遍认同建构主义的教学理念，9 成以上的教师都认同教学应重视自主探究、主动思考和思维推理过程。其中，上

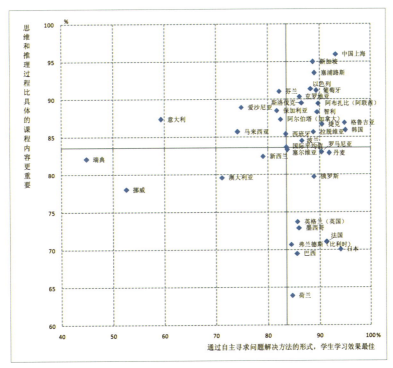

图 15　教师对建构主义教学理念的认同

海教师认同"思维和推理过程比具体的课程内容更重要"的占
96.0%，认同"在教室向学生展示某个实际问题如何解决之前，应
该先给学生思考解决方式的机会"的占 98.7%，均是所有国家和地
区中认同度最高的。

新加坡教师除了在"通过自主寻求问题解决方法的形式，学
生学习效果最佳"方面认同度（88.7%）低于上海外，其他几方面
均与上海非常接近。国际平均而言，教师在 4 项理念上的认同度
介于 83.6% 至 94.2% 之间。

2. 常用多种教学策略

2.1 总结内容与检查作业

上海初中教师最常用到的教学策略是总结近期学过的内容
和检查学生的练习本或家庭作业，在所有或几乎所有课上应用

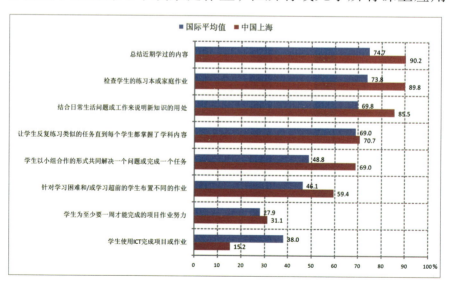

图 16   经常运用各项课堂教学策略的教师比例

的教师比例分别达 90.2% 和 89.8%，相应的国际均值为 74.7% 和 73.8%。其中，上海教师运用总结内容教学策略的比例是所有国家（地区）中最高的一个。新加坡运用这一策略的教师仅占 67.2%。新加坡教师最常使用的策略是检查学生的作业，经常运用的教师比例达 83.6%。

2.2 联系实际说明新知识的用处

上海教师报告经常结合日常生活问题或工作来说明新知识的用处，比例达 85.5%，相应的国际均值 69.8%，新加坡教师运用这一策略的比例更低，仅为 60.6%。

2.3 小组合作学习

小组合作学习是积极教学策略（包括小组合作学习、长作业和运用 ICT 完成作业）的一项重要内容，有 69.0% 的上海教师经常使用这一策略，是三种策略中被运用最多的。同时，小组合作学习也是绝大多数国家（地区）教师常用的教学策略。在这方面，上海与东亚的韩国、日本、新加坡显著不同，这些国家经常运用小组合作学习的比例均在 30% 左右。

2.4 反复练习

尽管反复操练被视为机械式的被动学习，但实际教学中，经常使用这种策略的教师仍比较多。TALIS 国际平均而言，69.0% 的教师经常采用这种方法。上海经常采用反复练习方法的教师达到 70.7%，与 TALIS 均值没有显著差异。新加坡教师使用这一策略为 67.5%，显著低于上海。值得注意的是，东亚的日本和韩国教师使用该策略比例最少，分别为 31.9% 和 48.0%。

3. 重视教学观摩和教学专业合作

3.1 教学观摩及反馈活动最多

在所有的教学合作活动中，99.0% 的上海教师都观摩其他老师的课堂并提供反馈，参与教师的比例是所有国家（地区）中最高的。其次是日本（94.5%）、韩国（93.9%）和俄罗斯（93.9%），新加坡的比例为 80.0%，而 TALIS 国际平均水平仅为 60.2%。

表 3　初中教师教学观摩及反馈活动的频率

观察其他教师的课堂并提供反馈的频率	国际平均值（%）	中国上海（%）	差异（百分点）
从未有过	39.8	1.0	38.8***
每年 1 次或更少	20.9	5.6	15.3***
每年 2–4 次	21.0	19.3	1.7*
每年 5–10 次	7.9	28.4	−20.4***
每月 1–3 次	6.3	34.3	−28.1***
每周 1 次或更多	4.1	11.4	−7.3***

注：* 表示差异达到 0.05 显著性水平；*** 表示差异达到了 0.001 显著性水平。

上海不仅进行教学观摩及反馈的教师比例最大，且活动频率也是所有国家中最高的。每月进行 1 次或多次教学观摩及反馈的教师占 45.7%，是接近该比例第二高的阿联酋阿布扎比和格鲁吉亚比例（24.4%）的两倍，TALIS 国际平均仅为 10.4%，新加坡教师进行教学观摩及反馈的比例与国际均值接近，每月 1 次或多次的仅为 9.6%。可见，上海教师教学观摩及反馈活动不仅参与面广而且强度非常大。

3.2 重视教学专业合作

TALIS 将教师之间的合作行为区分为专业合作行为与简单交流和合作行为。前者是指在教师在教学方面深层次的合作活动，包括教学观摩与反馈，与其他教师上同一节课，参与跨班级或年级和合作活动，参与协作式的专业学习等。后者是指教师间较浅层的合作活动，例如教师与同事交换教学资料，讨论特定学生学习计划、共同确定评估标准和参加团队会议。

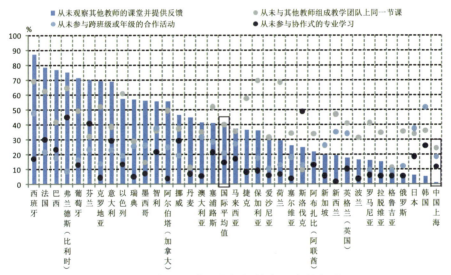

图 17　各国（地区）教师的专业合作行为

在专业合作指数上，上海的指数显著高于 TALIS 平均，尤其是前述的教学观摩及反馈活动上海教师表现尤为突出。相应的，在简单交流合作方面，上海教师的指数显著低于 TALIS 平均，尤其是"参与涉及特定学生学习发展计划讨论"的教师比例不足80%，与韩国一起是比例最低的两个国家（地区）。在新加坡，无论专业合作还是简单交流，指数均显著高于 TALIS 均值。

4. 学生评估方法

4.1 学生个别回答问题、为学生写评语运用较多

在所有国家（地区）中，上海教师经常使用学生个别回答方式的比例是最高的，达 86.8%，超过 TALIS 国际平均 35.2 个百分点，比新加坡高 22.4 个百分点。

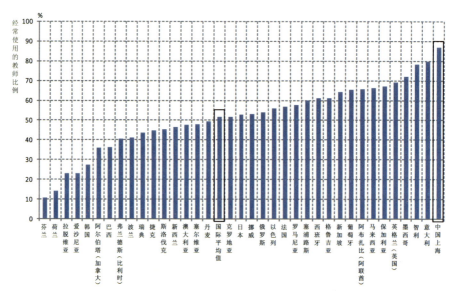

图 18 各国（地区）教师报告经常"让学生在全班同学面前个别回答问题"的比例

此外，上海教师在打分或评定等级外为学生写反馈意见的比例占 70.6%，高出国际均值 16.1 个百分点，新加坡的比例比上海略高，为 72.5%。两者都属于运用比较多的国家（地区）。

4.2 标准化测试使用较多

有 66.2% 的上海教师报告经常使用标准化测试，而经常使用

自编测试的教师占 55.9%。与上海类似，经常使用标准化测试的新加坡教师占 70.5%，与拉脱维亚一起同属比例最高的国家（地区）。但新加坡教师经常使用自编测验的比例为 64.7%，虽然低于 TALIS 平均的 66.4%，但却远高于上海的比例。

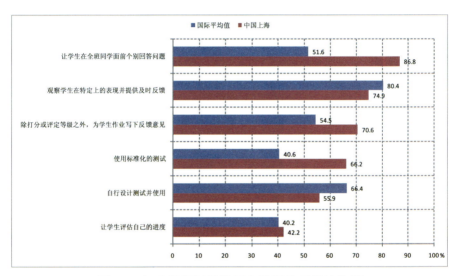

图 19　初中教师经常使用各种评价手段的比例

4.3　观察学生在特定任务上表现并及时反馈低于国际平均

国际平均而言，观察学生在特定任务上的表现并及时反馈是教师最常使用的评价方法，教师比例达到 80.4%，在马来西亚、智利、阿布扎比、墨西哥、新西兰和澳大利亚，报告经常采用这一方法的教师都超过 90%。

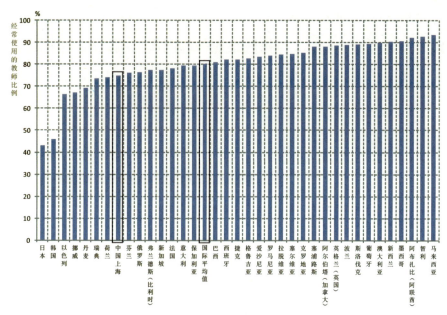

图20 各国（地区）教师报告"观察学生在特定
上的表现并提供及时反馈"的比例

上海教师经常使用这种评估方面的教师占 74.9%，同属东亚的日本和韩国教师经常使用这一方法的比例是最低的，均不足 50%，新加坡教师使用这种方法的比例为 77.5%，略高于上海。

五、对教师的评价

1. 学校管理人员和校长都是评价反馈的主体

上海教师得到评价反馈的比例达 98.4%，与英格兰、马来西亚和新加坡同属比例最高的国家（地区）。88.9% 的上海教师得到学校管理人员的评价反馈，45.7% 的教师得到校长的评价反馈，可见，学校管理人员和校长是上海教师评价和反馈的主要来源。新加坡与上海非常类似，得到学校管理人员和校长反馈的教师比例分别为 82.6% 和 50.4%。而 TALIS 国际平均来看，得到校长反馈的教师最多，占 54.7%，其次是学校管理人员，占 52.4%。

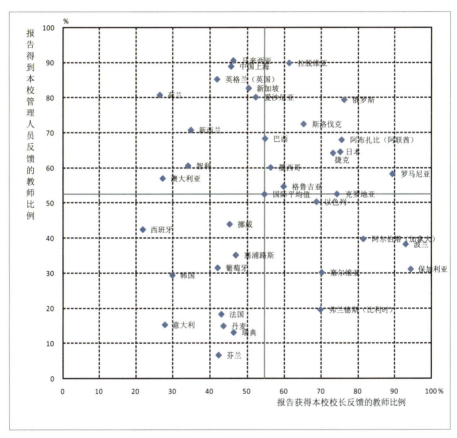

图 21　教师得到学校管理人员和校长评价反馈的比例

2. 多种评价反馈方式并重

在所有对教师的评价反馈方式中，观察课堂是上海最常见的，这也是绝大多数国家的共同之处。上海 95.7% 的教师报告会得到这种方式的评价反馈。该比例在新加坡是 96.8%，TALIS 国家（地区）平均而言，81.3% 的教师报告得到这种方式的评价反馈。

分析学生成绩、进行教师自我评价以及根据学生调查结果对教师进行评价反馈的方式在上海学校中也比较普遍，均有 80% 以上的上海教师报告。相对而言，新加坡学校较多采用教师自评的结果（87.2%），而较少采用学生调查的方式。TALIS 平均而言，报告这几类评价反馈方式的教师均在 55% 至 66% 之间。

总体而言，上海学校的教师评价反馈方式多样，并且各种方式应用的比例都远超 TALIS 各国平均。可见上海学校对教师评价反馈的重视程度。

3. 评价反馈的关注点

TALIS 国际平均而言，教师认为评价反馈注重较多的有学生成绩、学科教学能力、学生行为和课堂管理、学科知识理解、学生评估实践、与其他教师的合作或协同工作、学生反馈，回答"比较

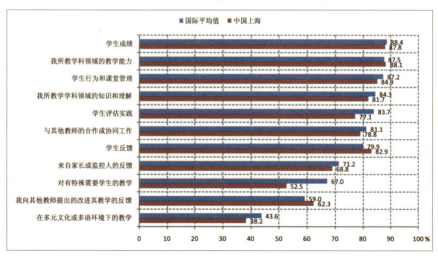

图 22　教师认为评价反馈中不同关注点受到重视的比例

注重"和"非常注重"的比例从 79.9% 到 88.4%。在大多数内容上，上海学校反馈的关注点都与国际平均比较一致。但上海教师反馈在注重评估实践、对特殊教育需要学生的教学以及多元文化或多语境下教学的关注较少。新加坡与上海的情况非常相似，并且在学生成绩、教学能力等主要关注点上比例更高。

4. 重视评价后的跟进工作

上海学校非常重视评价后的跟进。9 成左右的上海教师指出学校会安排带教老师帮助教师提高教学水平，学校会与教师讨论改进教学不足的措施。此外，82.2% 的教师指出学校会制定教师发展和培训计划。这些都显著高于国际平均水平。在这方面，新加坡也与上海类似，但绝大多数跟进措施的比例都略少于上海。

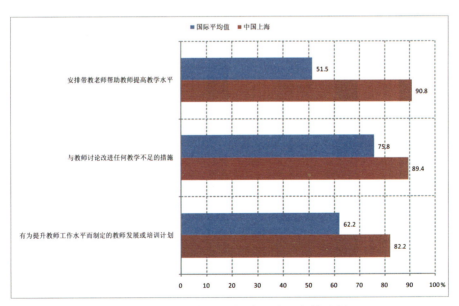

图23 教师经常使用各种评价手段的比例

六、教师教学时间、教学环境和社会支持

1. 工作时间——上课最少，改作业、辅导学生很多

上海初中教师每周工作时间（39.7 小时）处于中等水平，用于教学的时间为 13.8 小时，仅占工作时间的三分之一，是所有国家（地区）中最少的。TALIS 平均而言，教师每周教学时间（19.2 小时）占到工作时间（38.5 小时）的二分之一。上海教师在批改学生作业（7.9 小时）、辅导学生（5.1）、参与学校管理方面（3.3）和与本校同事合作交流（4.1 小时）上花费的时间高于大多数国家（地区）。尤其是前两项的时间远高于国际平均值。

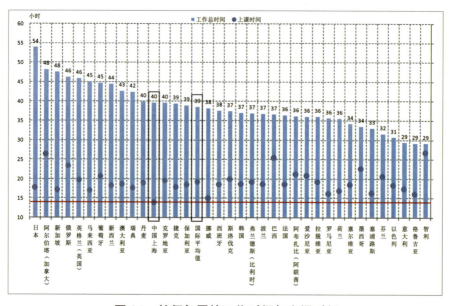

图 24 教师每周的工作时间与上课时间

新加坡教师每周工作时间达 47.6 小时，上课时间 17.1 个小时，两者都显著多于上海教师。在其他方面，新加坡教师用于学

生辅导的时间（2.6 小时）相对较少，但用于课外活动的时间（3.4 小时）相对较多。

国际总体来看，在除了上课之外的其他事务中，教师花费时间比较多的是个人规划备课和批改学生作业，平均时间分别为 7.2 和 5.0 小时。

2. 课堂时间——教学最多，纪律和管理最少

上海教师课堂时间的利用效率是所有 TALIS 参与国家（地区）中最高的一个。上海教师课堂时间的 86.1% 用于实际教学，远高于 TALIS 国际平均的 79.8%。相应地，上海教师用于维持课堂纪律和管理任务的时间分别为 7.9% 和 6.0%，均低于的 TALIS 国际均值 13.1% 和 7.9%。新加坡教师课堂约有三分之一的时间用于维持纪律和管理任务，属于课堂时间效率较低的国家。

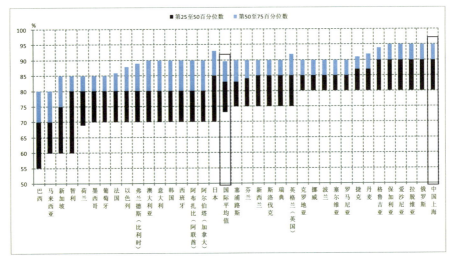

图 25　各国（地区）教师课堂用于教学的时间比例

分析表明，在绝大部分国家（地区），一半的老师都把课堂80%以上的时间用于实际的教学，而上海将80%的时间用于教学的老师达到3/4，同时，上海有一半的老师将90%的时间用于教学，而在大多数国家，该比例为80%至85%。

3. 课堂纪律风气良好

与PISA结果一致，上海教师认为其课堂纪律风气良好。在有关课堂纪律风气的4项描述中，3项列TALIS国家（地区）第一位，1项列第二位。总体而言，9成左右上海教师都认为课堂纪律风气良好。

TALIS平均而言，大约四分之一的教师认为课堂纪律风气不好。在这方面，新加坡教师的看法更消极，有三分之一左右的教师认为课堂纪律风气不好。

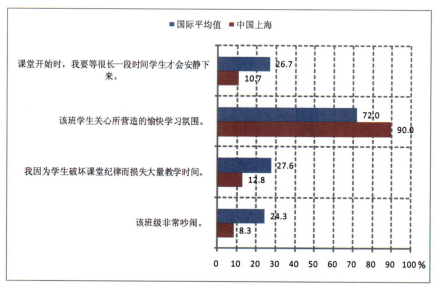

图26 教师对"目标班级"的纪律状况的看法

4. 学校师生关系融洽

96.3% 的上海初中教师认为学校师生关系融洽，97.6% 的教师关心学生的健康成长，认为学校重视学生意见、能提供额外帮助的教师比例在 93% 左右。相比上海，有更多新加坡教师认为学校能为有需要的学生提供额外帮助，比例达 98.3%。TALIS 平均来看，认同上述各项的教师比例均在 9 成以上。

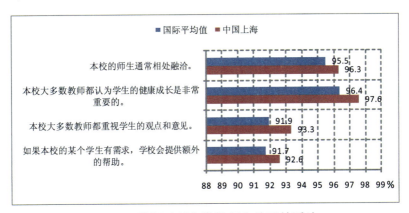

图 27　教师对所在学校师生关系的看法

5. 教师自我效能感与国际平均持平

TALIS 用 12 个问题从课堂管理效能感、教学效能感和学生参与效能感三个方面调查了教师的自我效能感情况。总体来讲，上海教师的工作效能感与 TALIS 国家（地区）平均水平没有显著差异。

上图显示了教师任教年数与自我效能感之间的关系。可以看到，教龄 20 年以内，上海教师任教年数越长，自我效能感越高，任教 16 至 20 年的教师效能感最高，超过 20 年任教年数的教师效能感变化不大。而 TALIS 平均而言，教龄越高，教师效能感越强，任教 30 年以上的教师，效能感最高。

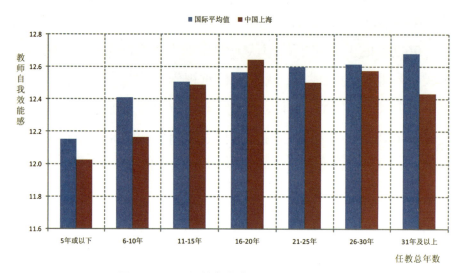

图 28　不同任教年数教师的自我效能感

6. 教师的工作满意度

6.1 认同教师职业受社会重视，但职业满意度低

上海教师认为教师职业受社会重视的比例达 45.3%，比 TALIS 国际均值高 12.9 个百分点。在这方面认同度较高的有新加坡（67.6%）、韩国（66.5%）、阿联酋阿布扎比（66.5%）和芬兰（58.6%）。

认同教师职业受社会重视的校长比例更高，TALIS 国际平均为 45.8%，上海有 71.6% 的初中校长认同这一看法。相对而言，在这个方面认同度最高的国家分别为新加坡（95.3%）、韩国（89.6%）和芬兰（78.6%）。其中，中国上海与芬兰在统计上无显著差异，可见对于 PISA 表现卓越的国家或地区而言，教师这个职业备受社会重视显然成为校长们的共识。

尽管认同教师职业受重视的比例超过 TALIS 平均，但上海教师对教师职业的满意度在所有 TALIS 国家（地区）中处于低端（还有瑞典和斯洛伐克）。在"我会向人推荐我们学校是个工作的好地方"这一选项上，仅有 60.6% 的上海教师表示认同，而 TALIS 平均而言，有 83.5% 的教师表示认同。在"我很享受在本校的工作"方面，上海教师认同的比例为 70.8%，而 TALIS 平均为 89.3%。在"如果给我再次选择的机会，我还是会选择当老师"一项上，上海教师认同的比例为 67.6%，而国际均值为 77.8%。

与上海相似，尽管教师认同职业受社会重视，但韩国、新加坡等国家教师对职业的满意度也显著低于 TALIS 平均。同为东亚国家的日本，不仅认同教师职业受社会重视的比例仅为 28.1%，教师对职业的满意度也显著低于 TALIS 均值。

6.2 满意自己在学校的表现，但对工作环境满意度最低

94.1% 的上海教师满意自己在学校的表现，显著高于 TALIS 平均的 92.4%，也显著高于新加坡（87.1%）、韩国（79.4%）、日本（50.5%）等国家。

但上海教师对当前学校工作环境满意度很低，与韩国同属满意度最低的国家和地区。在具体项目上，仅有 60.6% 的上海教师认同"我会向人推荐我们学校是个工作的好地方"，有 30.5% 的教师在考虑换一所学校工作。日本、新加坡教师对工作环境的满意度也属于最低的行列。

第三部分：上海 TALIS 的校长调查结果

一、上海初中校长概况

1. 年富力强，女性约占 1/3

上海初中校长的平均年龄约为 49 岁，与国际平均水平相当。从年龄分布看，超过一半的上海初中校长（55.1%）不足 50 岁，小于 40 岁的校长占 3.4%，大于 60 岁的校长占 6.8%。可见，校长队伍并未出现老龄化问题。日本和韩国校长队伍老龄化问题比较突出。

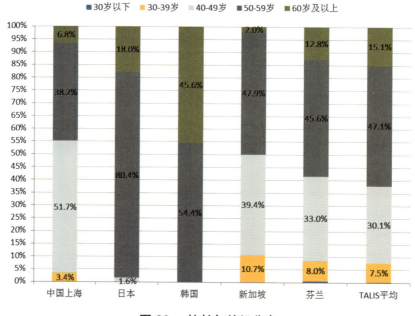

图 29　校长年龄组分布

在上海，女性任初中校长的比例为 38.6%，低于 TALIS 平均值（49.6%）和其他一些 PISA 表现卓越的国家（地区），如新

加坡（52.5%）和芬兰（40.6%），但显著高于日本（6%）和韩国
（13.3%）。

2. 学历水平高但具有博士学历的校长不多

在上海，接受过大学本科及以上水平教育的初中校长占
98.6%（其中，大学本科学历的校长占81.9%，硕士研究生学历占
16.7%），还有0.8%的校长具有博士研究生学历。从TALIS平均
水平看，92.8%的初中校长接受过本科和硕士研究生教育，3.2%
的校长具有博士研究生学历。

3. 教龄长，管理经验丰富

无论校长接受过何种层次和内容的教育或培训，工作经验在
对校长行为和态度的塑造上具有不可替代性。TALIS调查校长问

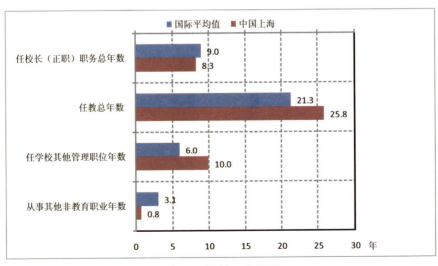

图30　校长工作经验

卷分别从校长的任职、教龄、学校管理岗位和从事其他非教育职业年数等方面综合描述校长的工作经验。

从数据结果发现，第一，上海初中校长教龄显著高于 TALIS 平均，上海校长平均有 25.8 年的教学工作经验，国际平均值为 21.3 年；第二，上海初中校长比其他国家或地区的初中校长拥有更丰富的管理工作经验，平均有 10 年从事其他管理岗位工作的经验，国际平均值为 6 年；第三，上海校长平均只有 0.8 年从事非教育职业的工作经历，国际平均值为 3.1 年。可见，上海初中校长在任职以前已经具备相对充分的教学和管理工作经验，且长期从事教育领域的工作。

4. 专业准备全面充足，教学领导力储备世界领先

在 36 个参加 TALIS 2013（包括 TALIS 2013+）调查的国家（地区）中，上海初中校长在正规教育阶段接受过学校管理或校长培训项目、教师培训 / 教育项目或课程、教学领导力培训或课程，这三项教育 / 培训内容的比例均最高且差异最小（见表 4）。

表 4　初中校长接受的正规教育中涵盖的培训内容

参加过的培训内容	中国上海	TALIS 平均值	差异百分比
学校管理或校长培训项目	99%	91%	8.0***
教师培训 / 教育项目	99.6%	85.6%	14.0***
教学领导力培训课程	97.9%	78.8%	19.1***

注：* 表示差异达到 0.05 显著性水平；** 表示差异达到了 0.01 显著性水平；*** 表示差异达到了 0.001 显著性水平

TALIS 调查根据校长是否或何时接受过上述三项培训内容的
不同回答（从未，任校长之前，之后，之前和之后），合成了校长领

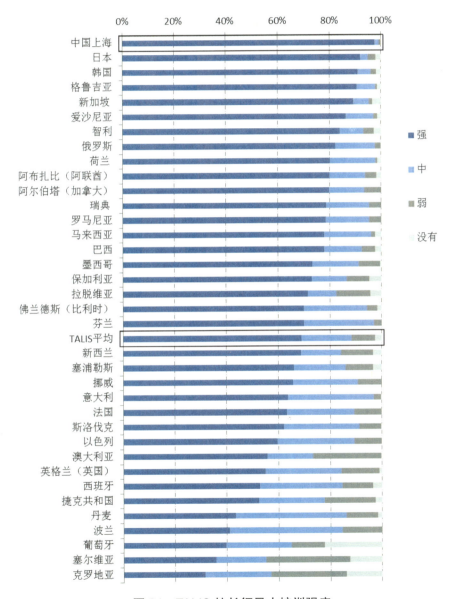

图31　TALIS 校长领导力培训强度

导力培训指数（PLEADERI），该指数为 0 则表示没有接受过领导力培训，1 表示接受的程度弱，2 表示接受的程度中等，3 表示接受的程度强。97.6% 的上海初中校长所受领导力培训的程度为强度，显著高于国际平均水平（68.8%），新加坡的该项比例为 89.2%。

二、校长的专业发展

TALIS 2013 调查把教师和校长的专业发展活动分为校内专业发展活动和校外专业发展活动这两大类，并分别对这两类活动的参与度和强度（最近 12 个月参与的天数）进行调查。其中校外专业发展活动是指参加学习课程、会议或考察访问；校内专业发展活动是指参加教研活动、带教或研究活动。

1. 校外专业发展活动

94.9% 的上海初中校长报告在最近 12 个月里参加过校外专业发展活动。该项参与率在 36 个参加 TALIS 2013 调查（包括 TALIS 2013+）的国家（地区）中排名第 2 位，仅次于新加坡（99.3%），国际平均为 83.3%。从持续的天数看，与其他国家或地区比较，上海的优势最大。94.9% 的上海初中校长报告，在最近 12 个月里参加过校外专业发展活动（学习课程、会议和考察）且天数为 39.5 天，在 36 个参加 TALIS 2013（包括 TALIS 2013+）调查的国家（地区）中持续的天数最长，国际平均为 13.6 天，新加坡为 13.4 天。

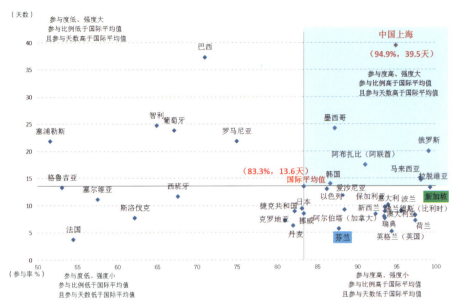

图 32　校外专业发展活动（学习课程、会议或考察）的参与和强度

2. 校内专业发展活动

92.4% 的上海初中校长报告在最近 12 个月里参加过校内专业发展活动。该项参与率在 36 个参加 TALIS 2013（包括 TALIS 2013+）调查的国家（或地区）中排名第 2 位，仅次于新加坡（92.5%），国际平均为 52.6%。从持续的天数看，与其他国家或地区比较，上海的优势最大。92.4% 的上海初中校长报告，在最近 12 个月里参加过校内专业发展活动并且天数为 39.1 天，在 36 个参加 TALIS 2013（包括 TALIS 2013+）调查的国家（地区）中持续的天数最长，国际平均为 20.7 天，新加坡 15.5 天。

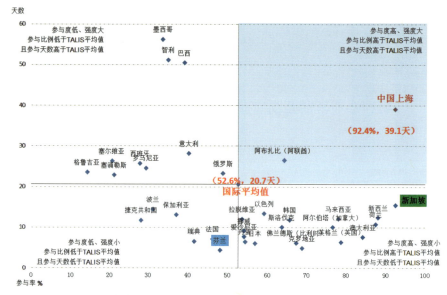

图33　校内专业发展活动（教研活动和带教）的参与和强度

三、校长的工作

1. 校长日常工作的时间分布

上海初中校长教学、行政双肩挑。TALIS 调查询问了校长平均 1 学年中日常工作的时间分配。调查结果发现，上海初中校长在课程与教学相关工作上投入了较多的精力，平均 1 学年在该方面工作上投入的时间比例在 36 个参加 TALIS 调查的国家（或地区）中排名第 1。

上海校长报告，平均 1 学年，33% 的时间花费在课程和教学相关工作及会议上，该项比例的 TALIS 平均值为 21.8%；相比之下，上海校长在行政管理事务上花费的时间比例为 34.9%，显著低于 TALIS 平均（41.5%）。

国际平均值

- 行政管理工作
- 课程和教学相关工作
- 与学生互动
- 与家长或监护人互动
- 与外界互动
- 其他

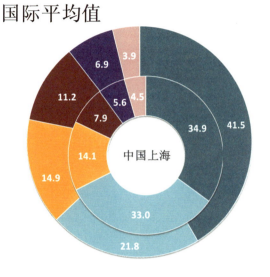

图 34　校长工作时间分布（%）

　　这从一定程度反映了，上海的校长是教学专家型的校长，并非是只专注于行政管理事务的行政型校长。这与校长准备教育阶段充足的教学领导力培训或课程的学习有一定关系。但 TALIS 调查还显示，上海初中校长与学生家长或监护人互动的时间比例为 7.9%，显著低于 TALIS 平均（11.2%）；与外界（如社区、企业等）互动的时间比例为 5.6%，也显著低于 TALIS 平均（6.9%）。这说明与国际平均水平相比，上海初中校长与外界的联系相对薄弱，领导力的影响范围有待进一步拓展。

2. 校长经常参与的事务

　　TALIS 调查询问了校长在最近 12 个月里经常参与了哪些事

务的情况。数据结果发现，促进教学和教师间专业协作是上海初中校长最为关注和投入精力去做的事务。

91.1%的上海初中校长报告，在最近12个月内经常或很经常地到课堂观察教师教学，该项的TALIS平均比例为52.3%；近90%的上海初中校长表示经常或很经常地采取行动支持教师间协作、确保教师提高教学技能和对学生结果负以责任。TALIS调查根据校长对上述3个问题的回答合成了校长教学领导力指数，该指数的标准差为2，中间点为10。上海初中校长的教学领导力指数（PINSLEADS）为12.1，显著高于国际平均值（11.1），与新加坡该指数相比无显著差异且位列36个参加TALIS调查国家（或地区）的第4。以上数据表明上海校长具有以专业引领和促进教师专业发展为核心的教学领导力特征。

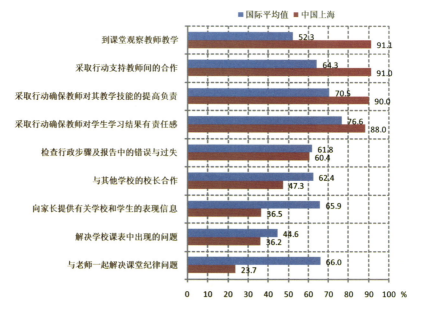

图35 最近12个月内校长经常或很经常参与的事务

第四部分：上海 TALIS 结果的讨论

一、上海调查结果显现的优势

1.“三位一体”的教师政策体系

改革开放以来，在基础教育教师专业发展方面，上海逐步形成了一个“三位一体”的教师专业发展体系：教师职称晋升体系、工作绩效评估和在职进修制度三者相互结合、互相推动，不仅从内部激发教师专业发展的动机，更从外部提供了有力的支持和激励，促使教师持续不断地提升自身专业能力，这成为推动上海基础教育质量提高最为重要的力量。

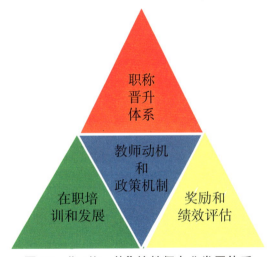

图 36 “三位一体”的教师专业发展体系

TALIS 数据表明，上海教师专业发展的参与广度和强度远超其他国家和地区，不仅如此，在几乎所有专业发展主题方面，上海教师的参与比例都高于国际平均水平。这些均显示了上海在教师专业发展方面所构建的政策体系所发挥的强大作用。

尽管世界各国大都非常重视教师的专业发展，然而，真正能建构起职称晋升、绩效评价和在职进修三者合一，形成合力的国家很少。在很多国家，基础教育阶段教师并没有职称晋升体系，或者教师晋升主要考虑其任教年限；大多数国家对教师的在职进修并没有明确的要求，也缺乏绩效评价的有效方法。这就会导致在很大程度上教师的职后发展主要依靠其专业自觉性。然而，个人的自觉性很难保障所有教师都参与到在职专业发展活动中，特别是伴随教师年龄增长和职业倦怠的出现，教师在职专业发展的动力会愈发弱小。这样一来，即使政府单方面提供丰富的专业发展活动也很难发挥应有的作用。甚至还有些国家，一旦发现教育问题，就拿教师做"替罪羊"，或者走向另一极端，完全"凭结果发工资"（pay by result）。

上海"三位一体"的政策体系既能有效发挥教师个人的专业自觉性，又能给予教师专业发展足够的支持和督促，还能不断为教师的努力提供正面反馈，可以保障绝大多数老师持续的专业能力提升，减少职业倦怠。

2. 扎根于学校、教师和教学的学校教科研制度

上海乃至中国学校中的教师专业发展活动，已经成为中国基础教育师资队伍建设最为鲜明的特征。OECD 在为上海推出的特别报告中指出"相比其他 TALIS 国家（地区），上海教师参加深度专业发展活动频率更高"。尤为突出的是，上海教师参加课堂观察

和协作式的专业学习的比例远高于国际均值。

上海教师在深度专业发展活动方面的突出表现与我们长期以来所坚持的学校教科研制度密不可分。这一制度可以追溯到20世纪50年代，到今天，已经形成了从政府到专业研究机构，再到学校和校内教科研小组的非常完善的组织。它也成为贯彻教育改革重大举措的核心机制。TALIS数据表明，四分之三的上海教师报告，学校教研组、备课组至少每两周活动一次。而在教研活动中，超过一半教师报告最常见的活动是听评课和集体备课。同时，对于学校科研，有接近9成的教师认为学校科研主题主要源于实际工作中遇到的问题，科研活动有利于提高教学水平，能够帮助学校总结教师的实践知识。

无论是上海学校的教研活动还是科研活动，其最鲜明的特征就是扎根于学校、教师和教学的实际和现场，即它们都是"校本"的。学校教科研制度为教师提供了信息沟通、经验分享、思想碰撞、情感交流的平台，成为上海教师专业发展最为重要的形式。上海学校教师的"教研组""备课组"和"年级组"已经被各国专家和教师誉为"最为有效的教师学习共同体"。

3. 教师专业发展受到政府和学校的全力支持

尽管认识到教师专业发展的重要性，但并非所有的国家和学校都能全力支持教师的专业发展。一方面，教师专业发展需要时间投入，而这必然会影响到教师工作时间的安排。在这方面，较少的实际教学时间为上海教师参与专业发展活动提供了良好的基础，保障了教师能有充足的时间进行个人和集体的专业发展活动。同时，上海市教委针对不同职业发展阶段的教师确定了专业发展的基本线，即见习期新教师专业发展要达到 120 学时，在职教师 5 年内必须达到 360 学时，而高级教师必须修满 540 学时。上海初中学校的校长对教师专业发展同样非常重视，93% 的上海初中学校校长都会为学校制定专业发展计划，这有力地保障了政策在学校层面的落实。TALIS 的结果表明，近 9 成的上海教师认为自己有固定时间参加工作时间内的专业发展活动，远远高于国际平均水平。

另一方面，教师专业发展活动需要大量经费投入。在教师培训方面，上海市政府持续加大投入，明确规定市区两级政府要确保培训经费的足额投入，在十二五期间，还规定学校要将生均经费 100 元投入教师培训中。除了对政府和学校规定的教师培训支持外，对于教师个人的在职教育类学位进修，政府也提供一定额度的学费补贴。这些措施有力地保障了教师专业发展的权利。TALIS 数据表明，上海有 80% 的初中教师认为，自己无须为专业发展活动付费，显著高于绝大多数国家（地区）。

可见，无论从时间还是经费上，上海教师在专业发展方面得到的支持力度都非常大。尽管如此，仍有近 6 成的上海教师指出，与工作时间冲突阻碍了其进行专业发展，有超过一半的教师认为专业发展缺少激励措施。可见，对教师的专业发展支持还需要更为细致周密的时间安排和更精准的激励配套措施。

4. 以开放的心态不断学习新理念和新方法

作为中国最早对外开放的城市，上海早已形成海纳百川的城市精神。这种开放包容的形态也鲜明地体现在上海的教育发展上，善于学习、敢于尝试、勇于创新也成为上海教育的显著特征。通过持续的国际交流与合作，上海教育界不断学习新的教育理念和方法，同时结合自身特点和实际状况，推陈出新，创造出具有上海特色的教育思想和实践，较早的如愉快教育、成功教育，近年以来的后茶馆教育、新优质学校、学业质量绿色指标等都是其中的典型案例。

TALIS 2013 的调查数据也清晰的体现出了这一特征。9 成以上的上海教师都认同建构主义的教学理念，并且认同"思维与推理过程比具体的课程内容更重要"和"在教室向学生展示某个实际问题如何解决之前，应该先给学生思考解决方式的机会"的教师比例居所有国家和地区首位。可见建构主义这一源自西方的教学理念在上海教师中的普及程度。PISA 测试也表明，上海学生对于记忆策略的运用显著低于 OECD 平均，而在精致策略方面与 OECD 持平，这显然与教师在教育理念方面的特征紧密相关。

5. 校长具有很强的教学领导能力

陶行知先生曾说过"一个好校长就意味着一所好学校"，而学校的首要工作就是教学，由此可见，校长的教学领导力对于一所学校的重要性。

TALIS 数据表明，几乎所有上海校长（97.9%）都在其正式教

育中完成了校长领导力培训，这比 TALIS 国家（地区）均值高 19
个百分点。这表明，相比其他国家和地区，上海校长在教学领导
力方面准备得更为充分。不仅如此，上海校长无论在校内还是校
外的专业发展活动方面，参与度和持续时间均是最高的国家（地
区）之一。这充分保障了校长对自己教学领导能力的持续关注，
也让他们更加重视学校的教学活动，愿意付出时间和精力。

　　TALIS 数据也体现了上海校长的这一特征。上海初中校长平
均有 33% 的工作时间投入在课程与教学方面，高出 TALIS 平均水
平 11 个百分点，而在行政工作方面，则比 TALIS 均值低 6 个百分
点。这表明，相比其他国家的校长，上海校长在其校长职责中更
为重视教学工作的地位。

二、上海调查结果给我们的启示

1. 关注教师和校长工作满意度，改善工作环境，增强教师对本职工作的认同

　　TALIS 数据分析表明，尽管绝大部分（86.9%）教师对自己的
工作总体满意，但上海教师对职业的满意度、当前工作环境的满
意度以及总体的工作满意度都是所有国家（地区）中比较低的。
同时，尽管大部分校长认同教师这项职业受到社会尊重，但他们
自己对校长这个专业身份的认同程度却并不高。另一方面，97.5%
的初中校长对自己的工作总体满意，但上海校长的职业满意度也
是比较低的。这需要特别引起我们的重视。

TALIS 数据分析表明，教师的工作满意度显著影响教师工作效能感。尽管这些都是教师的主观感受，但这些主观感受必然会潜移默化地影响到教师教育教学诸多方面。因此，如何进一步提高中小学教师职业地位，提高教师总体收入和绩效性收入，改善学校的工作环境，建设一支积极向上、爱岗爱生、专业化的教师队伍是上海亟待解决的问题。

2. 关注学生多样性方面的教师专业发展需求

随着市民对教育质量要求的逐步提高，学生群体的逐步多元，特别是"为了每个学生全面发展"的教育追求，上海教师应更重视学生多样化的需求。TALIS 调查发现，尽管上海教师已经非常关注个性化学习方面的专业发展，但在不同语言、多元文化下教学的专业发展活动、针对特殊需要学生教学的专业发展活动以及学生职业生涯指导方面的专业发展活动都比较少，仍有待加强。尽管在不同语言、多元文化方面，上海当前面临的群体不大，但农民工子女的教育却是我们需要特别关注的。在教师的专业发展活动中需要特别针对这一群体的教学进行内容设置。

正在开展的上海市高校招生考试改革，特别是从"唯分数高低"一本、二本、高职高专的填报志愿的方法，转变为关注学生个性特长和未来职业生涯发展的"按个性擅长"填报高校志愿的改革，也从另一维度推动着教师必须关注学生个性发展，学会认识和发现学生个性，培养学生兴趣和潜能，关注学生在不同的成长阶段予以有效的辅助和引导。

3. 加强 ICT 和教学场所新技术的应用

随着近年来对教学相关 ICT 技术（信息交流技术）的重视，这方面的培训力度逐步增强。过去一年上海参加 ICT 方面专业发展活动的教师占 63.9%，教师需求的比例也达到 67.2%，两者均超过了 TALIS 国际均值。尽管如此，上海教师经常要求学生使用 ICT 完成项目和作业的比例非常低，仅为 15% 左右，仅为新加坡一半，大大落后 TALIS 国际均值，差异达到 22.8 个百分点。

另一方面，TALIS 平均而言，教学相关的 ICT 和教学场所的新技术是教师专业发展需求中最多的两项，比例达 59.5% 和 56.1%，而尽管分别有 67.2% 和 44.3% 的上海教师也需要这方面的发展活动，但相比其他专业发展内容，需求的教师比例偏低。

尽管 ICT 和新技术的教学应用在不同国家（地区）间离散程度很大，也没有发现使用 ICT 越多学生成绩就越高的确凿证据。但随着信息化和新技术对人们工作、生活方式的改变，随着我们的学生成为 ICT 和大数据时代的"原住民"，学生们在未来学习、工作和生活中将越来越多地使用和依赖 ICT 和大数据，因此教育理念和方法的变革是必然的。如何让教师在思想上做好准备，在技术手段上得到训练，在教学资源和管理工具上得到供应，从而将 ICT 和新技术融入教育教学中，真正使现代最新技术为教育教学服务，为因材施教服务，为学生的个性化学习服务，这是我们在专业发展活动中需要努力加强的。

4. 考虑调整学校辅助人员配比

上海初中校长所在学校，辅助人员的配备明显不足，尤其是教学辅助人员的数量显著低于其他 PISA 表现卓越的教育体系，如新加坡、芬兰、日本等；并且教学辅助人员短缺对提供优质教学构成问题，这已成为影响校长工作满意度的显著因素。

上海初中学校生师比为 11.3，显著低于国际平均水平（12.3）。与国际平均水平相比，上海教学辅助人员和管理辅助人员还不够充足，尤其是教学辅助人员的配比。上海初中教师与管理辅助人员的配比为 11.0，该项比例的国际平均值为 6.3，芬兰为 8.2，新加坡为 2.7。这表明，在上海初中，平均 1 名管理辅助人员支持 11 名教师。更为严重的是，上海初中教师与教学辅助人员的配比为 21.6，该项比例的国际平均值为 14.7，新加坡 11.9，芬兰 12.4。这表明，在上海初中，平均 1 名教学辅助人员支持 22 名教师，约为管理辅助人员工作量的 1 倍。从 PISA 测试表现卓越的教育体系看，如新加坡、日本、韩国、芬兰和荷兰等国家，上述两项比例的平均值均低于国际平均值并且低于上海平均值。这说明，上述国家或地区的这两类辅助性人员的数量都要比上海充足。

此外，需要注意的是，在控制了校长年龄、性别和受教育水平等因素后，对校长工作满意度与学校资源短缺进行回归分析后发现，缺少辅助人员对教学构成问题与校长工作满意度显著负相关。这说明改善辅助人员短缺问题有助于提高校长工作满意度。

5. 降低校长专业发展活动门槛，加强校长与社会互动

校长参加专业发展活动的门槛设置过高，不利于促进每一名校长的专业发展。"与工作时间冲突"（26.2%）、"不符合参加的基本要求"(12.5%) 和"没有激励措施"(10.9%)，这三项是上海初中校长提及最多的制约其参加专业发展活动的因素。其中，与国际平均值相比，认为"不符合参加的基本要求"的上海校长比例较高，且这一比例高于其他所有参与 TALIS 2013 调查的国家或地区。

上海初中校长在与学生、家长或外界互动的时间较少，显著低于国际平均值。TALIS 2013 调查了校长平均一个学年中日常工作的时间分配。上海初中校长在与学生互动（14.1%），与家长互动（7.9%）、与外界互动（5.6%）这些工作上花费的时间均比国际平均值要低。这说明校长与社会和社区的联系还是比较薄弱的，主动从外界获得教育资源和支持的意识和能力较低，需进一步加强校长这方面能力建设，使每所学校都能够在社会各界的理解和支持中得到更好的发展。

后　记

　　"教师教学国际调查"（TALIS）是上海继"国际学生评估项目"（PISA）后参与的又一大型国际教育测评研究项目。在本轮研究报告付梓之际，我们研究团队最感激的是为了完成这项研究付出了辛劳和努力的所有同志！如果没有市教委领导的高瞻远瞩和资金提供，没有市教委人事处、外事处、财务处、基教处等各个处室全力支持，没有上海师范大学对我们研究工作的充分理解，没有上海所有区县教育局、招生办、信息办等机构的认真配合，没有200所抽样中学、4000多位校长、教师不厌其烦在指定时间内上机回答问卷，这样大规模、高标准、国际化的调查是无法实施的！而上海初中教师在国际调查中所表现出的令世界各国瞩目的结果，更是集中反映了改革开放三十多年来上海师资队伍建设的成就！集中体现了上海广大教师敬业爱生、精益求精和终身发展的精神！上海中小学教师、上海教育界的同事们，我们课题组在获得了研究数据后，更加由衷地敬佩你们！

　　本项研究由张民选主持，依托上海师大国际与比较教育研究院完成。本研究报告亦由张民选负责策划、主编、确定研究结论。朱小虎撰写第一、第二和第四章，第三章由徐瑾劼撰写，张民选审阅全书并对书稿做了修改。在书稿付印之时，我们还要感谢上海教育出版社，特别是童亮和周吉编辑，正是因为你们的工作，才能使本报告与读者见面。

张民选

2017 年 3 月 10 日

Professionalism and Excellence

A Brief Report of the Teaching and Learning International Survey 2015 in Shanghai

Shanghai TALIS Center

上海教育出版社
SHANGHAI EDUCATIONAL
PUBLISHING HOUSE

TALIS International Institutes:

Organisation for Economic Co-operation and Development (OECD, Paris, France)

TALIS International Consortium :

International Association for the Evaluation of Educational Achievement (IEA, Amsterdam, Netherland)
Data Processing and Research Center of International Association for the Evaluation of Educational Achievement (IEA DPC, Hamburg, Germany)
Statistics Canada (Ottawa, Canada)
Australian Council for Educational Research(ACER, Melbourne, Australia)

Organization Institutions of Shanghai Project:

Steering Committee of TALIS Project, Shanghai Municipal Education Commission
Research Institute for International and Comparative Education, SHNU
Shanghai TALIS Secretariat / Research Center

Contact Us:

E-mail : talis_shanghai98@vip.163.com
Address : Room 1102, Jiao Yuan Building,
Shanghai Normal University,
No. 100 Guilin Rd., Shanghai

Contents

Part One: An Overview of Shanghai TALIS

I. An Introduction to OECD TALIS

The Organisation for Economic Co-operation and Development (OECD) has discovered in PISA that, apart from family and parents, teachers are the most influential factor to students' academic achievements and growth. Therefore, governments around the world are obliged to improve teacher policy and enhance teacher professionalism. However, the reality is less satisfactory. Angel Gurria, OECD Secretary-General, has pointed out:

"The skills that students need to contribute effectively to society are in constant change. Yet, our education systems are not keeping up with the fast pace of the world around us. Most schools look much the same today as they did a generation ago, and teachers themselves are often not developing the practices and skills necessary to meet the diverse needs of today's learners."

With the purpose of understanding teacher policies and professional development status as well as identifying positive practices and promoting teachers development in all countries, OECD has organized and conducted the Teachingand Learning International Survey (TALIS) since 2008 after the launch of the Programme for International Student Assessment (PISA).

1

Currently, TALIS is the international teacher survey that has the largest scale, attracting the greatest number of participating countries. It focuses on the working conditions for teachers, the professional development of teachers, and the learning environment of schools. By collecting and analyzing reliable, timely, and comparable data, TALIS hopes to help countries (regions) to create a professional education team by reflecting on their education policies and formulating quality policies.

In 2008, 24 countries (regions) participated in the firstcycle of TALIS, providing information on lower secondary school teachers and principals. Later in 2009, TALIS issued its inaugural report, *Creating Effective Teaching and Learning Environments*: *First Results from TALIS*.

From 2013 to 2014, a new round of TALIS survey was carried out in 34 countries (regions) across the world. Meanwhile, OECD arranged a TALIS 2013+ survey specifically for four new participating countries (regions), and one of them was Shanghai. Except for the time differences (TALIS 2013+ completed in the first half of 2015), TALIS 2013+ adopted the same survey scope and technical specifications as TALIS 2013. Hence, the survey results of over 110,000 participating teachers and principals from 38 participating countries (regions) are comparable.

Teaching and Learning International Survey (TALIS) mainly uses survey questionnaires to collect data from principals and teachers. The questionnaires are designed by OECD entrusted professional institute and are implemented upon approval of the Council of participating countries. According to OECD requirements, all participating countries (regions) shall have 20 teachers and 1 principal from 200 lower secondary schools to take part in the survey. OECD uses international sampling guidelines and international tools to select teachers and schools across the world. At present, TALIS has extended its teacher survey to upper secondary and primary schools. Except the core teacher survey for lower secondary schools, participating countries enjoy the autonomy to decide whether to participate in surveys for primary schools and/or upper secondary schools.

TALIS includes two sections, which are teacher survey and principal survey (Table 1). The teacher survey consists of 52 questions spanning 7 themes, namely background information, teachers' professional development, teachers feedback, teaching in general, teaching in target class, school climate, job satisfactory and overseas training. The principal survey contains 41 questions covering 8 different themes which are individual profile, professional development, school profile, school leadership, teachers' formal appraisal, school climate, teachers' induction and mentoring programmes, and job satisfaction. Apart from the distinctive contents of either survey, there is also cross-evidencing content in both surveys.

To better understand the status quo of the participating countries and regions, OECD allows all respondents to add several national questions in the surveys. Hence, Shanghai structured the survey to suit its local context by adding 3 questions on professional development in the teacher survey and 2 questions on background information in the principal survey.

Table 1   Analysis on Themes and Questions of Shanghai TALIS 2013+Questionnaires

	Themes	Number of Questions	Content
Teacher Questionnaire	Background Information	18 (1–18)	Gender, age, teaching experience, employment status, classroom climate, pre-career education, working time
	Teacher's Professional Development	12 (19–30, 51–52)	Type of induction programmes, type, time, theme distribution, and impact of professional development activities, support, method, need of and barriers to professional development activities,

(continue)

	Themes	Number of Questions	Content
Teacher Questionnaire			frequency, content, form and reflection of teaching and research activities, overseas training programmes
	Teacher Appraisal and Feedback	4（31–34）	Source of feedback, content of feedback, impact of feedback and reflection on feedback
	Teaching in General	3（35–37）	Philosophy, collaboration, and competency of teaching
	Teaching in Target Class	9（38–46）	Class composition, teaching subjects, number of classes, class time allocation, discipline, teaching tactics, evaluation methods
	School climate and Job Satisfaction	4（47–50）	Decision-making, student-oriented, job satisfaction, individual characteristics

(continue)

	Themes	Number of Questions	Content
Principal Questionnaire	Personal Background Information	7 (1–7)	Gender, age, work experience, educational attainment, professional preparation
	Principal's Professional Development	3 (8–10)	Professional development activities (participation rate, intensity), barriers to professional development activities
	School Background Information	7 (11–17)	Location, public/ private, school competitiveness, size of student body, ratio of specific student groups, school resources
	Principal's Leadership	10 (18–28)	Working time allocation of principals, instructional leadership, work barriers
	Teachers Formal Appraisal	3 (29–31)	Subjects, frequency, and feedback of the appraisal

(continue)

	Themes	Number of Questions	Content
Principal Questionnaire	School climate	3（32–34）	School clomate, teacher-student relationship, factors affecting instructional competency, discipline
	Teachers Induction and Mentoring	6（35–40）	Induction programmes, format of induction programmes, mentoring, principal's perception on the significance of mentoring programmes
	Job Satisfaction	1（41）	Principals satisfaction towards working environment, principal's satisfaction towards the profession

II. Rationale of Shanghai's participation in TALIS

Apart from their families, schools are the most important places for students' development. It cannot be denied that, among various school factors, teachers are the most influential factor. For example, judging from Shanghai students' excellent performance on the three

7

major subject areas in PISA 2009 and PISA 2012, it is evident that their teachers must have played a critical role. Although Shanghai PISA 2012 and Shanghai TALIS 2013+ are different in terms of samples and time of completion, both of their results have reflected the overall situation of basic education in Shanghai.

Amidst the worldwide heated debate on education in Shanghai, researchers at home and abroad inevitably focus their interests on Shanghai teachers. How does Shanghai select and train its teachers? How do Shanghai teachers work, learn and develop? These all became the topics of concern for visiting researchers from different countries.Through TALIS, we can learn more about the features of the teaching profession in Shanghai on an international platform and summarize the successful experience of Shanghai teaching profession development. On the other hand, there are some shortcomings and deficiencies underlying the great accomplishments achieved in the basic education sector and these issues rely on the cause identification and pedagogical reforms from the teachers and teaching perspective. In this regard, TALIS can also provide us with helpful inspirations and references which can then serve as cohesive evidence for Shanghai when compiling the 13th Five-Year Educational Plan as well as further promoting the scientific decision-making in education.

Lastly, participating in such international teacher survey helps us gain an in-depth understanding and learning of the current methodology, techniques and practices in the field of teacher research. This in turn will boost the construction of a multi-dimensional teacher evaluation system in Shanghai teachers.

III. Project structure of Shanghai TALIS

Shanghai Municipal Education Commission (SMEC) decided to participate in TALIS 2013+ in April 2014. The programme was led and supervised by Deputy Director of the Municipal Education Commission, Mr. WANG Ping, with Prof. ZHANG Minxuan from the Research Institute for International and Comparative Education of Shanghai Normal University serving as the National (regional) Project Manager.

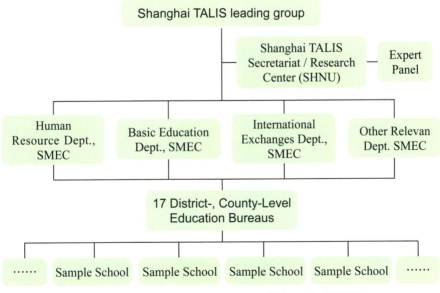

Figure 1　The project structure of Shanghai TALIS

The Secretariat and Research Center were established under the Research Institute for International and Comparative Education, SHNU.

The implementation of TALIS calls for coordination between various departments including the Human Resources Department, Basic Education Department, and International Exchanges Departments from SMEC, as well as support and collaboration from 17 district- and county-level education bureaus before eventually conducting it smoothly in every sample school.

IV. Samples and participation rates of Shanghai TALIS 2013+

The sampling of Shanghai lower secondary school teachers strictly follows TALIS technical standards and adopts a two-stage stratified sampling method. At the initial stage, PPS(Probability Proportionate to Size Sampling) was used to select school sample. School location and status (public or private)were used to stratify Shanghai schools. The second stage is teachers ampling within the sampled schools on a random basis.

On 1 January 2015, 3925 teachers from 199 lower secondary schools (independent lower secondary schools, 9-year continuum schools, and lower secondary sections of full secondary schools) across Shanghai participated in TALIS 2013+, representing the total number of 36628 lower secondary school teachers in Shanghai.

Meanwhile, 196 principals from the participating schools completed the principal questionnaire.

Table 2   Sample and representation of Shanghai TALIS

Explicit Type	Number of Sampled Schools	Number of Not Participated Sample Schools	Number of Participated Sampled Schools	Number of Participated Teachers	Number of Participated Principals
Public-Urban	70	1	69	1333	68
Public-Suburban	90	0	90	1795	87
Private-Urban	16	0	16	320	15
Private-Suburban	24	0	24	477	23
Total	200	1	199	3925	193

After the weighted calculation, the participation rate of Shanghai schools reaches 100%, with a 99.0% participation rate for the teachers and thetotal participation rate of 99.0%, demonstrating a very good representation.

Chapter Two: Teacher Survey Results of Shanghai TALIS

I. An Overview of Shanghai lower secondary school teachers

1. Distribution of teachers' age and teaching experience

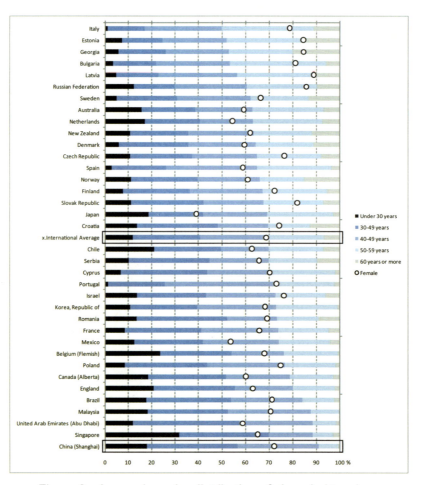

Figure 2　Age and gender distribution of shanghai teachers

The average age of Shanghai lower secondary school teachers is 38, which is 5 years younger than the international average. They are the youngest group second only to Singapore among all the TALIS participating countries and regions. Judging from age groups, Shanghai teachers are primarily at their 30s and 40s, with a joint proportion of 73%. Young teachers under 30 years old account for 17.9% of the total while those between 50 and 60 account for an even lower percentage of 9.1%.

Though the lower secondary schools in Shanghai boasts a very young group of teachers, the average teaching experience of them are not short, with an average of 15.5 years, just one year less than the TALIS international average of 16.5. Across all the countries (regions), Singaporean teachers enjoy the youngest average age, two years younger than Shanghai average. Meanwhile, Singaporean teachers

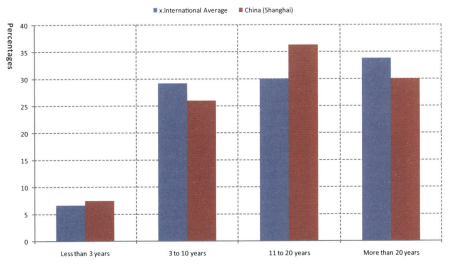

Figure 3   Teaching experience distribution of shanghai teachers

13

are also the less experienced ones with only 9.7 years of teaching experience on average.

As shown in Figure 3, Shanghai teachers with 11 to 20 years of working experience accounts for the largest proportion, which is 36.3%, followed by a 30.1% of teachers boasting over 20 years of teaching experience. When it comes to TALIS average, the largest percentage, 36.0%, goes to teachers with no more than 10 years of teaching experience. Those with more than 20 years of teaching experience come in the second place occupying 33.9% of the total. The remaining teachers account for the least significant number (30.1%). Across all participating countries (regions), Singapore enjoys the greatest proportion of teachers with no more than 3 years teaching experience (20.4%) while a 68.2% of teachers have no more than 10 years of teaching experience, which indicates the country has a very young team of teachers.

2. Gender distribution of the teachers

As indicated by Figure 2, all TALIS countries (regions) have more female teachers than male counterparts with Japan being the only exception. Statistics of international average suggests a 68.8% of female teachers. The percentage for Shanghai is even higher, reaching 72.2%. This indicates that females remain the majority of teachers in most countries (regions).

14

Interestingly, though females account for a remarkably higher proportion than the male counterparts in most countries (regions), a notable low percentage of women principals is seen in almost all TALIS participating countries (regions).

II. Pre-career education and induction programmes of teachers

1. Distribution of teachers' educational attainment

In Shanghai, 98.5% lower secondary school teachers have

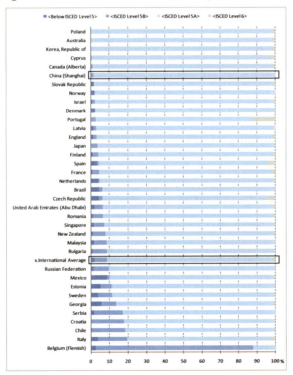

Figure 4　Educational attainments of lower secondary school teachers

15

received undergraduate or above education (among whom 89.4% have bachelor degrees and 9.1% have master or doctor degrees), reflecting that the Shanghai lower secondary school teachers boast a relatively high educational attainment. The TALIS international average for lower secondary school teachers having received undergraduate or above education is 91.2%. Singapore exceeds slightly by 92.7% in this regard.

In countries (regions) such as Portugal, Czech, and Spain, there is a relatively higher ratio of lower secondary school teachers acquiring a doctoral degree. Shanghai, in contrast, only has a mere 0.05% of doctoral teachers in lower secondary schools.

2. Teachers' education and training

TALIS regards teacher education and training programmes as teachers' professional training. While the international average is merely 90.4%, Shanghai remains a relatively high achiever in this aspect. 98.2% of Shanghai teachers have completed teacher education or training programmes, almost at the same level as that in Singapore (99.1%).

Generally, Shanghai teachers believe that the teacher education or training they received is relatively comprehensive. Only a small portion of teachers think that the content of subject(s) (1.2%), pedagogy of subject(s) (2.1%), and the classroom practice (4.9%) including practicum, internship or teaching student in their teaching subjects are not included drespectively. However, 2.8% of Singaporean

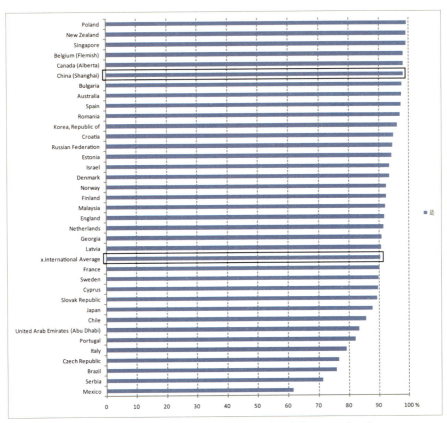

Figure 5   Teacher education and training received
by lower secondary school teachers

teachers reported an absence of content of subject(s), which is higher than Shanghai. But in terms of classroom practice components, Singapore enjoys a better situation with only 1.6% of its teachers reporting of non-coverage. As for pedagogy (1.8% for Singapore), there's no significant difference.

3. Teachers' confidence in professional preparedness

Teachers' professional preparedness reflects the confidence

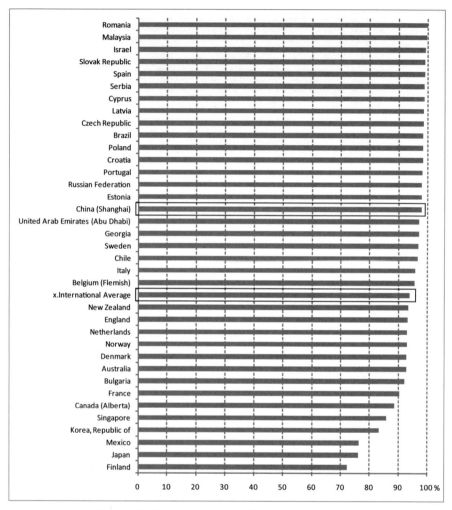

Figure 6   Preparedness of teaching contents

a teacher holds against his/her teaching content, pedagogy and classroom practice.

Regarding the content of teaching subjects, 97.9% of Shanghai teachers are confident that they prepare well or very well while the international average remains at 93.9%, which indicates a higher

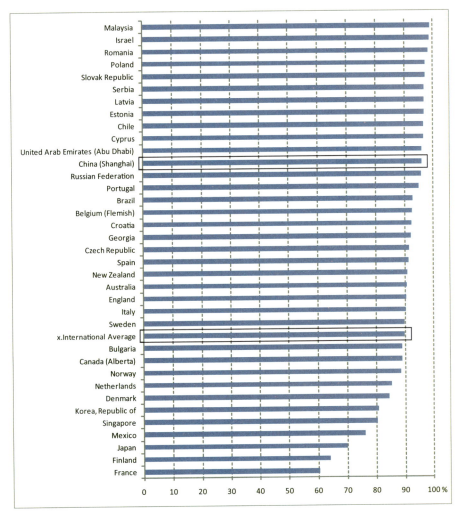

Figure 7   Pedagogy preparedness of teaching subjects

confidence level of Shanghai teachers on teaching content than their

international counterparts.

Regarding the pedagogy of the teaching subjects, 96.0% of

the Shanghai teachers believe that their preparation is well or very

well.With the figure being significantly higher than the international average of 89.7%, it shows a greater confidence among Shanghai

teachers on pedagogy.

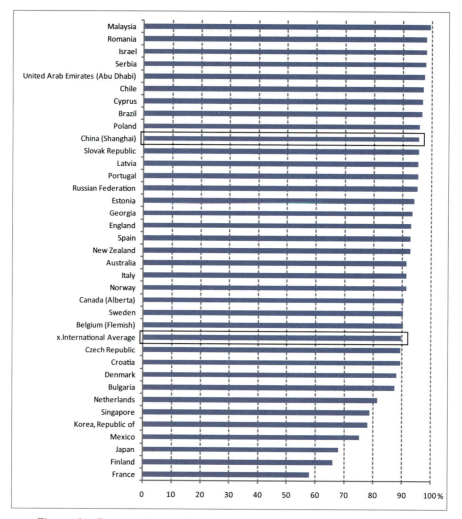

Figure 8   Preparedness of classroom practice in teaching subjects

Regarding the classroom practice in the teaching subjects, 95.4%

of the Shanghai teachers are confident that they prepare well or very

well while the international average remains at 89.5%, which again indicates a higher confidence level of Shanghai teachers on classroom practice than their international counterparts.

In general, based on the three indicators of teachers' preparedness of their teaching subjects, the majority respond positively, which reflects the professional confidence level of Shanghai teachers to some extent.

4. Participation of induction activities by new teachers

Almost all schools (99.2%) in Shanghai provide formal induction trainings to teachers. Meanwhile, about nine tenths (89.0%) of the

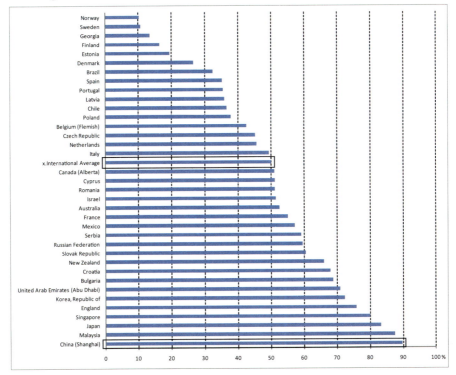

Figure 9   Reported participation rates of formal induction activities

teachers reported participating in formal induction activities. Schools in Singapore (100%) and England (99.4%) all provide teachers with formal induction activities. However, the reported participation rates, 80.0% and 75.8% respectively, are significantly lower than that in Shanghai.

99.7% of teachers with no more than three years of work experience are provided with formal induction training by their schools and their participation rate in such activities is 97.4%. In Singapore, 100% of the schools offer formal induction activities while the participation rate is 96.9%.

5. Mentoring programmes among teachers

All schools (100%) in Shanghai provide teachers with mentoring programmes while the international average only remains at 70%. In Singapore and England, mentoring programmes are also widely provided in almost every school.

According to the principals, the mentors and the mentees teach exactly the same subject in most cases in all the lower secondary schools (100%) in Shanghai. However, the international average is only 69.5% and Singapore result is 85.5%.

Shanghai teachers witness a remarkably higher participation rate than the international average in mentoring programmes with 23% of the teachers report that they are assigned a mentor and 29.8% of the teachers report that they are assigned a mentee. The international

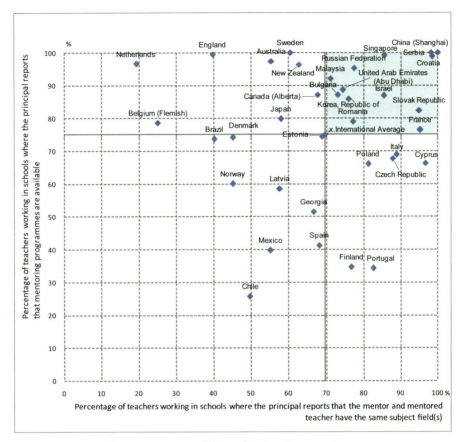

Figure 10   Subjects compatibility of school mentoring programmes

averages are 13.2% and 14.9% respectively. Singapore enjoys an even higher number for these two indicators, which are 39.6% and 39.4% respectively. This is probably linked to the abundant number of young teachers in Singapore.

III. Characteristics of teachers' professional development activities

1. High participation rate of professional development activities

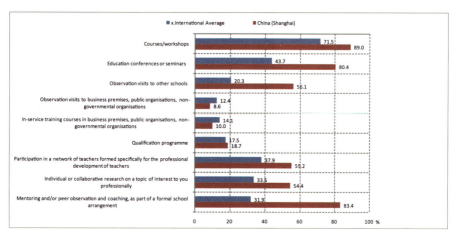

Figure 11   Percentages of teachers participating
in professional development activities in the last 12 months

97.7% of the Shanghai lower secondary school teachers have participated in some professional development activities during the past year, standing at the high ranks with Singapore (98.0%) and Alberta, Canada (97.7%) in this regard. When comes to the international average, the participation percentage drops to 88.7%.

Among various professional development activities, the most popular ones are "courses / workshops", "mentoring, peer observation and coaching", "education conferences or seminars", each enjoying participation rate over 80%, higher than the international average.

2. Great intensity of professional development

Shanghai teachers spend 62.8 days (equaling working days for 3 typical months) out of a year participating professional development activities while the international average is only 27.6 days. Similar cases are observed in Brazil (68.8 days) and Georgia (61.3 days) where teachers also have more than 60 days devoted to professional development. On the contrary, Flanders in Belgium, Norway, England, Sweden and Finland are the least dedicated countries (regions) in this regard which have less than a fortnight of professional development.

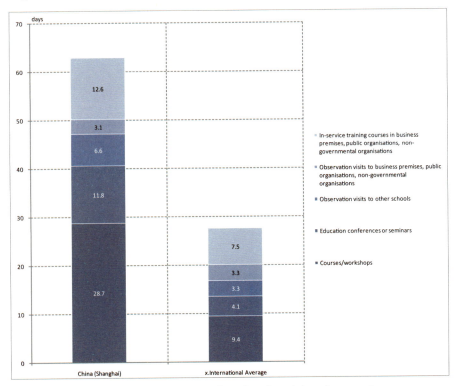

Figure 12   Duration of professional development
ctivities participated by teachers in last 12 months

25

In Singapore, the number reaches to 21.6 days.

When breaking down to specific activities, the time spent on courses and workshops is 28.7 days while that on in-service training courses in business premises, public organizations, or non-governmental organizations is 12.6 days and that on educational conferences and seminars is 11.8 days, all above the international level.

3. Highest participation rate in curriculum and instructional training activities

Among all the professional development activities that Shanghai

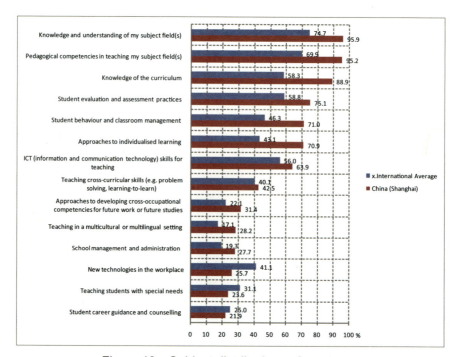

Figure 13   Subject distributions of teachers'
professional development activities

teachers participated over the last 12 months, 95.9% are about "knowledge and understanding of the teaching subjects", 95.2% focuses on "teaching competency of teaching subjects", and 88.9% covers "curriculum and knowledge", far higher than the international average of 74.7%, 69.9%, and 58.3% respectively. In comparison with Shanghai, Singapore scored 8-10% lower in all these activities.

4. Emphasizing individualized learning approaches

70.9% of Shanghai teachers reported having professional development activities on approaches to individualized learning during the last 12 months, ranking first in the survey. Besides, most of the Shanghai teachers chose approaches to individualized learning as the professional development area they need. The percentage reaches at 75.1%, In this regard, Singapore has a completely different situation where only 39.1% of the teachers participated in such activities, lower than that of the international average of 43.1%. Furthermore, the demand for professional development in the area of individualized learning approaches is also significantly lower than that of Shanghai, the percentage is only 57.8%.

When it comes to other areas of professional development focusing on diverse and differentiated teaching methods, Shanghai only sees a moderate percentage between 20% and 40%. Nevertheless, the participation rates in areas focusing on "teaching in multicultural or multilingual setting" (28.2%), "cross-curricular skills" (42.5%), "cross-occupational competencies for future work or studies" (31.4%) and "school management and administration" (27.7%) all surpassed the TALIS international average.

It is worth noting that the least attended activities were about "students career service", "teaching for students with special need", and "new technologies in teaching", with a reported percentage of 21.9%, 23.6%, and 25.7% respectively, which is 15.4, 7.5, and 3.0 percentage points lower than the respective international averages. Moreover, Shanghai teachers are also less demanding in new teaching technologies and teaching for students with special needs, compared to the international average.

5. Supporting teachers' professional development with time and incentives

Analysis shows that teachers' participation in professional development activities grows with the support of having scheduled time for such kind of programmes by countries (regions). The Shanghai survey suggests that 87.8% of teachers believe they do have time to participate in professional development activities during working hours. A similar high percentage is obtained for Malaysia (88.0%) as well, making the two countries (regions) the top two in this regard. However, in Singapore, the percentage is 70.3% while the

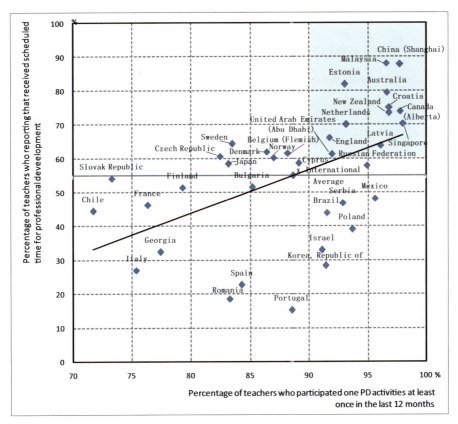

Figure 14   Participation rates in relation to having
scheduled time for professional development activities

international average is even lower, only 54.9%.

In terms of financing support, 89.7% participating teachers in Singapore reported that professional development activities are free to them, second only to England that enjoys a 92.7%. By comparison, 80.4% Shanghai teachers also reporte no payment for professional development activities, but the figure is smaller than other 10 countries (regions) such as England, Singapore, and others.

The primary barriers identified for Shanghai teachers remain as "conflict with working time (58.6%)", "lack of incentives (51.6%)", and "conflict with family responsibilities (40.3%)".

IV. Teachers' teaching characteristics

1. Recognizing constructivist teaching philosophy

The constructivist teaching philosophy is widely recognized by

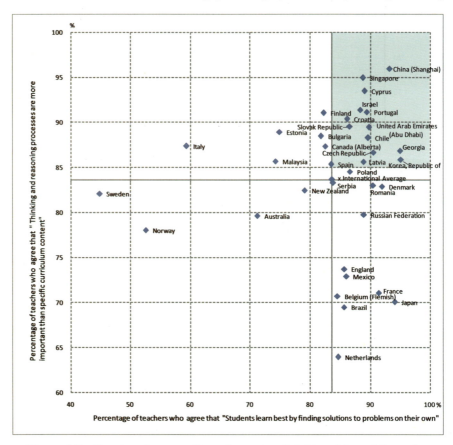

Figure 15   Teachers' recognition of constructivist teaching philosophy

Shanghai teachers with nine out of ten teachers believing that education needs to focus on independent inquiries, active thinking, and reasoning. Among them, 96.0% believe "thinking and reasoning are more important than specific course content" while an even higher percentage, 98.7%, agree that "teachers shall give students opportunities to think prior to simply presenting solutions to them", surpassing all other participating countries (regions).

Shanghai and its counterpart, Singapore, share similar results in all aspects except when it comes to the belief that "students obtain the best learning outcomes through independent problem solving" with Singapore reported an 88.7% of support. For all the four aspects surveyed, the international average renders between 83.6% and 94.2%.

2. Frequent use of multiple teaching methods

2.1 Summary of learned content and homework checking

The most frequently used methods by lower secondary school teachers in Shanghai are summary of recent learned content and checking students' exercise books or homework, which enjoys a percentage of 90.2 and 89.8 respectively, meanwhile, the international averages are 74.7% and 73.8%. The percentage of teachers who always use the method of summarizing the learned content in Shanghai is at the top of the international list.While in Singapore, 67.2% teachers always use the summary method, and for them, the most frequently used method is checking students' homework (83.6%).

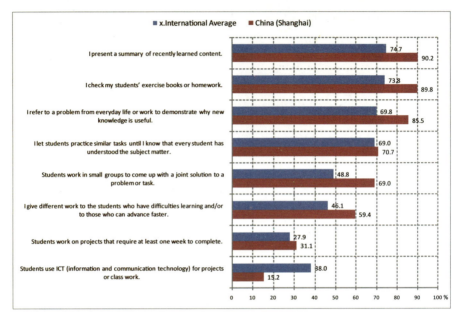

Figure 16   Percentages of teachers frequently using teaching methods

2.2 Demonstrating the usefulness of new knowledge in everyday life

While the international average sitting at 69.8%, 85.5% of Shanghai teachers report frequent references to everyday life or work to demonstrate the usefulness of new knowledge and only 60.6% teachers in Singapore reported adoption of this method.

2.3 Collaborative learning in groups

Learning in groups is an important way of positive learning methods (including collaborative learning in groups, long term student project or assignment, and homework through ICT) and is frequently adopted by 69.0% of Shanghai teachers, making it the most popular among the three discussed methods. The method is also widely practiced by teachers in a vast majority of the countries (regions). In this regard, Shanghai is significantly different from other East Asian countries such as Korea, Japan and Singapore, the proportion for which is only about 30%.

2.4 Repetitive exercises

Though repetitive exercises are regarded as passive learning, in real teaching practice, there are still a large number of teachers applying this method to their teaching. Looking at TALIS international average, 69.0% of teachers frequently use this method in their classes. When it comes to Shanghai, the number is only slight different, reaching 70.7%. However, in Singapore, this percentage drops to 67.5%, notably lower than that of Shanghai. It is worth noting that, the lowest percentages are witnessed in Japan and Korea where only 31.9% and 48.0% of teachers adopt this practice.

3. Emphasizing classroom observation and professional collaboration

3.1 Highest participation rate in classroom observation and feedback

Among the whole range of activities, 99.0% of Shanghai teachers report that they have observed other teachers' classes and provided feedback, boasting the highest participation rate across all participating countries (regions), followed by Japan (94.5%), Korea (93.9%) and Russia (93.9%). For Singapore, the ratio is 80.0%, while TALIS international average is only 60.2%.

Table 3   Frequency of classroom observation and feedback by lower secondary school teachers

Frequency of observing other teacher's class and providing feedback	International average (%)	Shanghai, China (%)	Difference (percentage point)
Never	39.8	1.0	38.8***
Once per year or less	20.9	5.6	15.3***
Two to four times per year	21.0	19.3	1.7*
Five to ten times per year	7.9	28.4	−20.4***
One to three times per month	6.3	34.3	−28.1***
Once a week or more	4.1	11.4	−7.3***

Note: *indicates a difference at 0.05 significant level; ***indicates a difference at 0.001 significant level.

As for classroom observation, Shanghai gets not only the highest participating rate, but also the highest frequency among all the countries (regions). More specifically, in terms of the ratio of teachers who observe at least one class per month, the proportion reaches 45.7%, almost doubles that of Abu Dhabi and Georgia (24.4%) who comes at the second place. When it comes to Singapore, 9.6% of the teachers participate in teaching observation activities once or several times per months, which is very close to TALIS international average (10.4%). Hence, the teaching observation activities in Shanghai are not only common but also very intensive.

3.2 Stressing professional collaboration in teaching

TALIS divides the collaboration between teachers into two categories, i.e. professional collaboration behavior and simple exchange and co-ordination between teachers. The former refers to the in-depth collaboration in teaching including classroom observation and feedback, teaching jointly as a team in the same class,

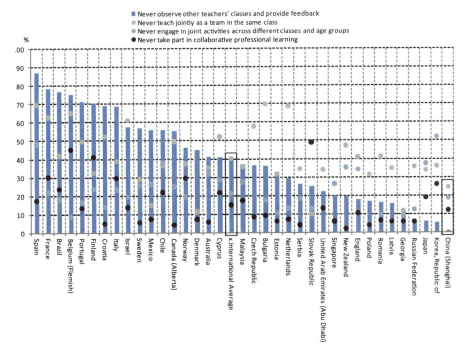

Figure 17   Teacher's professional collaboration behaviors

engaging in joint activities across different classes and age groups, and collaborative professional learning. On the other hand, the latter refers to the superficial collaboration behaviours such as exchanging teaching materials with colleagues, having discussions about students, ensuring common evaluation standards or attending conferences.

Comparing the indicators of professional collaboration, Shanghai performs much better than the TALIS average, especially in classroom observation and feedback. In contrast, Shanghai is below the TALIS average when it comes to simple exchange and co-ordination behavior. In particular, less than 80% of the Shanghai teachers took part in the "discussion of learning and development plan of specific students", bottoming the survey list with Korea. Singapore enjoys a remarkably better participation rates in both professional and communicative collaborations than TALIS averages.

4. Assessment methods of students

4.1 More practices of student answering questions individually and providing written feedback for students

Across all participating countries (regions), Shanghai teachers often asks individual students to answer questions, topping the TALIS list with 86.8% which is 35.2 percentage points higher than the TALIS average and 22.4 percentage points higher than that of Singapore.

In addition to grading and rating the students, Shanghai teachers

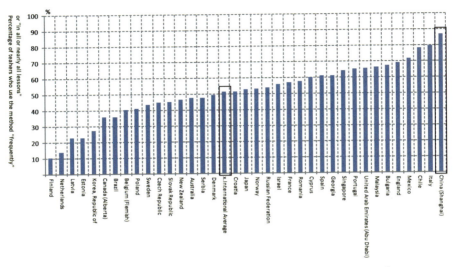

Figure 18   Percentage of teachers reporting frequent use of "asking
individual student to answer questions in front of the whole class" method

also write comments for the students and the percentage stays at 70.6%, which is 16.1 percentage points higher than the international average while 1.9 percentage points lower than that of Singapore. Singapore and Shanghai both are regions which have a larger proportion of teachers using this method.

4.2 Frequent application of standardized tests

There are 66.2% of Shanghai teachers suggesting that they use standardized tests very often while 55.9% using self-designed tests, which is similar to the situation in Singapore whereby 70.5% of teachers use standardized tests. Shanghai, together with Latvia, ranks the first by this indicator. However, in terms of the application of self-designed tests, though Singapore only boasts a percentage

of 64.7, lower than the TALIS average of 66.4%, its figure remains
significantly higher than that of Shanghai.

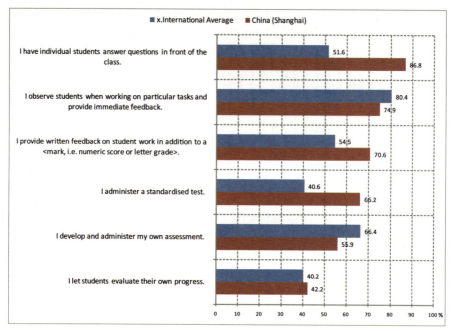

Figure 19   requently used evaluation methods by lower
secondary school teachers

**4.3 Lower than the international average in terms of observing
students' performance in specific tasks and providing timely
feedback**

According to the international average, observing students'
performance in specific tasks and providing timely feedback is the
most frequently adopted way of student evaluation by 80.4% of
teachers. In Malaysia, Chile, Abu Dhabi, Mexico, New Zealand and
Australia, this number even exceeds 90%.

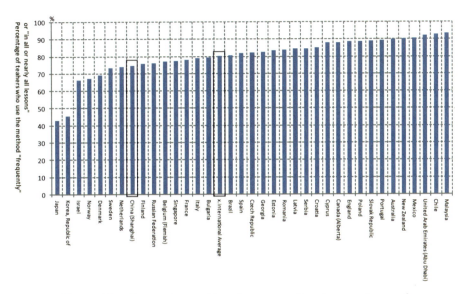

Figure 20   Percentage of teachers reporting frequent use of "observing students' performance in specific tasks and providing timely feedback for students" method

The proportion of teachers using above discussed method of evaluation reaches 74.9% in Shanghai while its counterparts in East Asia, Japan and Korea, see a lower than 50% of their teachers adopting this. In Singapore, there are 77.5% of teachers practicing this way of student evaluation, slightly higher than that of Shanghai.

V. Teachers' appraisal

1. School management team members and principals are the main source of teacher feedback

98.4% Shanghai teachers receive feedbacks, which is one of the highest among all countries (regions) along with England, Malaysia and Singapore. In Shanghai, 88.9% receive feedbacks from the school management team, while 45.7% receive from their principals, with which evidences that school management team and principals are the main source of teachers' feedbacks. Similar to Shanghai, Singapore sees 82.6% of teachers receiving feedbacks from school management team and 50.4% from principals. However, according to TALIS average, 54.7% teachers receive feedback from principals, which is a little higher than the percentage of teachers receiving feedback from school management team, namely 52.4%.

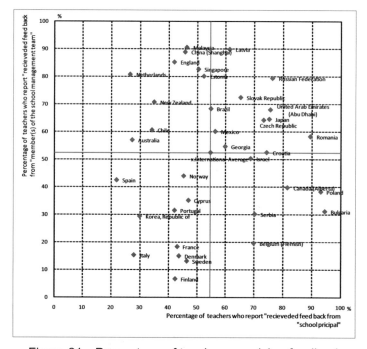

Figure 21   Percentage of teachers receiving feedback
from school management team and principals

2. Placing emphasis on multiple appraisal methods

Classroom observation is the most popular way of teacher appraisal and feedback in Shanghai and around the world. 95.7% of Shanghai teachers report receiving feedback following the direct observation of classroom teaching, while 96.8% of teachers in Singapore and 81.3% teachers on average among TALIS countries (regions).

Other popular ways of teacher's appraisal are analyzing students' test scores, self-assessment of teachers, and students' survey responses, each having an above 80% coverage. By comparison, Singaporean teachers are more frequently evaluated based on teachers' self-assessment (87.2%) rather than students' survey results. For TALIS average, around 55% to 66% of teachers experience all the above ways of appraisal.

In general, teacher's appraisal in Shanghai adopts various means and the percentage of each means all exceeds TALIS international average. This indicates that schools in Shanghai attach importance to teacher evaluation.

3. Focus of teachers' feedback

In terms of TALIS international average, 79.9% to 88.4% of teachers believe that the appraisal mainly focuses on student's performance, pedagogical competencies of teaching subjects, student behavior and classroom management, knowledge and understanding

41

of teaching subjects, student assessment practices, collaboration or working with other teachers, and student feedback. The conditions in Shanghai are quite similar in most of the aspects. However, when it comes to the student assessment practices, teaching of students with special needs, and teaching in a multicultural or multilingual setting, Shanghai teachers believe that less attention is paid to these elements. Singapore also experiences similar situations with Shanghai while a higher percentage of teachers believe that emphasis is placed on student's performance and pedagogical competencies.

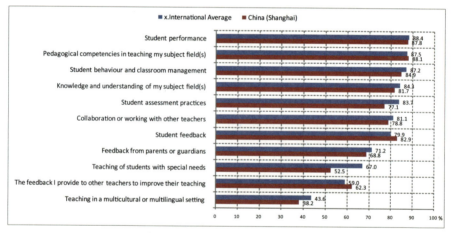

Figure 22   Different focuses of teachers' appraisal

4. Emphasizing post-feedback follow up

Schools in Shanghai attach extremely high importance to post-feedback follow up since around 90% of teachers indicated that the school will implement measures such as arranging mentors for them and discussing weaknesses with them to improve their teaching after the feedback. Moreover, 82.2% of them revealed that schools will create development and training plans for them. In this regard, Shanghai's performance is superior to the international average. For Singapore, the situation is similar as Shanghai, but the majority of the percentages related to follow-up measures are slightly lower than those of Shanghai.

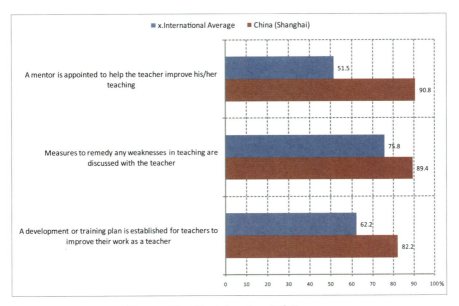

Figure 23   Post-feedback follow up

VI. Teaching time, environment and social support

1. Working time—least time for classroom teaching, more time for correcting homework and tutoring students

On average, secondary school teachers in Shanghai work 39.7

hours a week with 13.8 hours, one third of their total working time, devoted to classroom teaching. In comparison with other countries (regions), though the average working time of Shanghai teachers is at a moderate level, the time for classroom teaching is the least. According to TALIS average, teachers spend 19.2 hours which equals to half of their total working hours (38.5 hours) on classroom teaching. For Shanghai teachers, it is reported that 7.9 hours are spent on correcting homework, 5.1 hours on tutoring, 3.3 hours on school management and 4.1 hours on collaboration and communication with colleagues. This reveals that Shanghai teachers are required higher

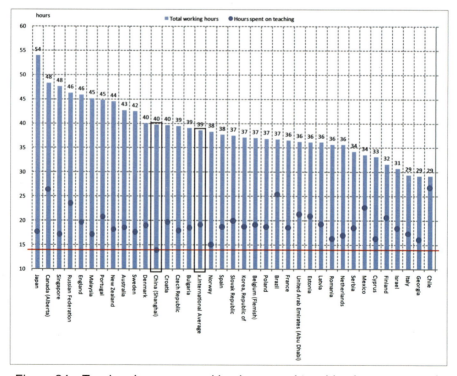

Figure 24   Teachers' average working hours and teaching hours per week

dedication in these four aspects in comparison with international average, particularly in the first two aspects.

In Singapore, the average teacher working time reaches 47.6 hours, among which 17.1 is dedicated to classroom teaching, both are remarkably longer than those of Shanghai. But Singaporean teachers spend relatively less time (2.6 hours) on tutoring students while more time (3.4 hours) on after-school activities.

As for the international average, apart from classroom teaching, teachers spend relatively more time on individual class preparation (7.2 hours) and correcting students' homework (5.0 hours).

2. Class time—teaching occupying the most, while discipline and management occupying the least

Highest efficiency of making use of class time is witnessed among Shanghai teachers amongst all TALIS participating countries (regions), where 86.1% of a teacher's class time is used for teaching. This goes far beyond the TALIS average of 79.8%. On the contrary, compared with the international average of 13.1% and 7.9% for keeping class order and administrative tasks respectively, Shanghai teachers only devote 7.9% and 6.0% of their class time to the above two aspects. Worse efficiency is identified in Singapore where around one third of the time is spent on these two tasks.

Analysis shows that half of the teachers spend more than 80%

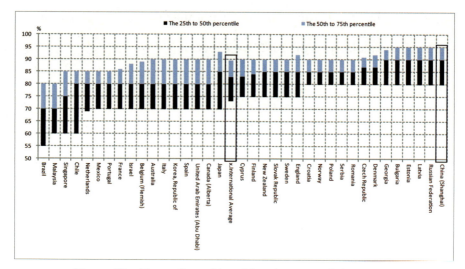

Figure 25   Proportion of teaching time out of class time

of their class time in teaching in most of the countries (regions), and in Shanghai, about 75% can do this. Furthermore, half of the Shanghai teachers spend 90% of their class time in teaching while the international average is only between 80% and 85%.

3. Good classroom disciplinary climate

In consistency with PISA results, Shanghai teachers regard the disciplinary situation in their classes as good. Three out of the four description items in disciplinary aspects suggest that Shanghai is the top of all TALIS participating countries (regions), while the remaining one indicates a second place for Shanghai. In general, 90% of the Shanghai teachers believe that the disciplines is good in their classes.

Compared with TALIS average which indicates around a quarter

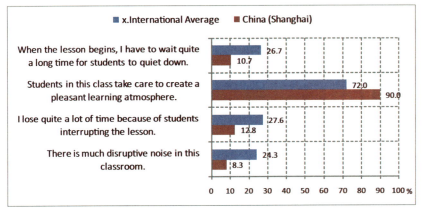

Figure 26   Teachers' perspective on disciplinary climate in "target class"

of teachers holding negative views on the classroom disciplinary situation, teachers in Singapore has an even negative view on this with the percentage reaching one-third.

4. Harmonious teacher-student relationship

96.3% of Shanghai lower secondary school teachers are confident

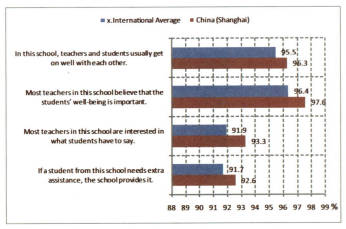

Figure 27   Teachers' perspective on teacher-student relationship of their schools

that they enjoy a harmonious teacher-student relationship. 97.6% of the teachers pay attention to students' well being, and 93% of teachers think that their schools are interested in students' opinions and can provide additional assistances students need.

5. Teachers' self-efficacy at the international average level

TALIS adopts 12 questions to study the self-efficacy level of teachers based on classroom management efficacy, teaching efficacy and students' participation efficacy. In general, no remarkable differences are noted in work efficacy of Shanghai teachers when comparing with TALIS international average.

The above chart reveals the relationship between teachers' self-efficacy and years of teaching experience. As evidenced in the chart, when the teaching experience is less than 20 years, the self-efficacy

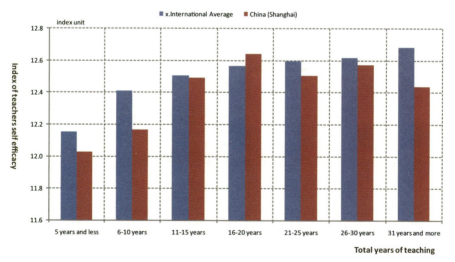

Figure 28   Self-efficacy of teachers, by teaching experience

grows with their teaching experience with a climax seen on teachers with 16–20 years of teaching. When the teachers have more than 20 years of experience, their self-efficacy becomes stable with no significant variations. Looking at the TALIS average, teachers' self-efficacy also grows with their seniority with a climax achieved when they have more than 30 years of teaching experience.

6. Job satisfaction

6.1 Low job satisfaction yet recognizing the profession as socially respected

45.3% of the Shanghai teachers agree that the teaching profession is respected by the society, 12.9 percentage points higher than that of the TALIS average. Greater recognition of this aspect is witnessed in Singapore (67.6%), Korea (66.5%), Abu Dhabi of United Arabic Emirates (66.5%) and Finland (58.6%).

The percentage of Shanghai principals who believe teaching profession is respected by the society reaches 71.6%, which is higher than that of the Shanghai teachers. For the TALIS average, 45.8% of the principals hold the same opinion. Highest percentages belong to Singapore (95.3%), Korea (89.6%) and Finland (78.6%). Shanghai is quite similar to Finland in this regard. This indicates that the principals have a consensus on the point that teacher is a highly respected profession in the society for countries (regions) which are high achievers in PISA.

Though a greater than TALIS average percentage of Shanghai teachers do recognize that teaching is socially respected, their job satisfaction is at the lowest level (accompanied by Sweden and Slovakia). Only 60.6% of Shanghai teachers say that they "would recommend my school as a good place to work", significantly lower than the TALIS average of 83.5%. Besides, 70.8% of Shanghai teachers believe that they "enjoy working at this school" when the TALIS average for this is 89.3%. Further more, 67.6% of Shanghai teachers say that they "would still choose to work as a teacher" if they could decide again, while the international average reaches 77.8%.

Countries such as Korea and Singapore share similar situations with Shanghai where the recognition of the profession remains prominent yet the job satisfaction stays lower than TALIS average. The other East Asian country, Japan, sees a mere 28.1% of teachers recognizing the profession is well respected in the society together with a below-TALIS-average job satisfaction.

6.2 Satisfied with self-performance at school while dissatisfied with the working environment

94.1% Shanghai teachers feel satisfied with their job performance, higher than the TALIS average (92.4%) and that of other countries such as Singapore (87.1%), Korea (79.4%), and Japan (50.5%).

Shanghai and Korea are regions where the lowest job satisfaction is seen. Specifically, only 60.6% of the Shanghai teachers agree that "the school I'm currently working for is a good place to recommend to others" and 30.5% of the teachers are thinking about changing a school to teach. Japan and Singapore also experiences the low job satisfaction.

Chapter Three: Principal Survey Results of Shanghai TALIS

I. An overview of principals in Shanghai secondary schools

1. Young and powerful, and 1/3 are females

The average age of principals in Shanghai secondary schools is around 49, comparative to the international average. A slightly over a half (55.1%) are younger than 50, while 3.4% are younger than 40 and 6.8% are older than 60. Therefore, aging problem is not identified among the principals in Shanghai, while the issue is comparatively prominent in Korea and Japan.

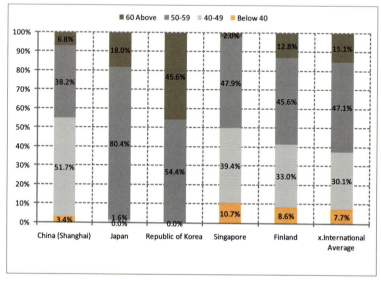

Figure 29   Distribution of principals' age group

On average, 38.6% of the principals in Shanghai are females, lower than the TALIS average of 49.6% and that of some PISA high achievers such as Singapore (52.5%) and Finland (40.6%), yet significantly higher than that of Japan (6%) and Korea (13.3%).

2. High education attainment but few Ph. Ds

98.6% of the principals in lower secondary schools in Shanghai received undergraduate and above education (among whom 81.9% are bachelors and 16.7% are masters) and 0.8% of the principals boast doctoral degree. In terms of TALIS average, 92.8% of the participating principals have received undergraduate and graduate education while 3.2% have enjoyed doctoral education.

3. Rich experience in teaching and management

Work experience plays an irreplaceable role in shaping principals' behavior and attitude regardless of what level or content of education or training principals have received. TALIS Principals Questionnaire takes a comprehensive look at the work experience of a principal from perspectives of tenure, teaching experience, and service length in school management or other non-educational professions.

Statistics reveal, firstly, lower secondary school principals in Shanghai are more experienced in teaching than TALIS average. In Shanghai, participating principals have 25.8 years of teaching

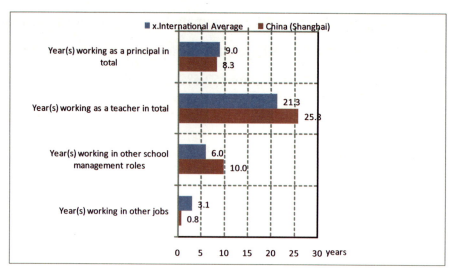

Figure 30   Principals' working experience

experience while the international average remains 21.3 years. Secondly, lower secondary school principals in Shanghai are also more experienced in management. On average, the respondents of Shanghai survey claim 10 years of work experience in other management positions while the international average is 6 years. Thirdly, in terms of work experience in non-educational professions, the international average suggests 3.1 years while that of Shanghai is only 0.8 years. In conclusion, the lower secondary school principals in Shanghai are equipped with sufficient teaching and management experience and have serviced in the education industry for a long time before taking office as a principal.

4. Comprehensive professional preparation, world-leading teaching leadership potential

Among all 36 participating countries (or region) of TALIS 2013 (including TALIS 2013+), lower secondary school principals in Shanghai boast the highest percentages in terms of receiving a) school management education or principals' training, b) teachers' training/education or courses, and c) teaching leadership training or courses during their full-time education period, and there are the least differences between these three figures.

Table 4   Training content covered in the formal education received by lower secondary school principals

Training content	Shanghai, China	TALIS average	Discrepancy by percentage
a) School management or principal programmes	99%	91%	8.0***
b) Teachers' training / education or courses	99.6%	85.6%	14.0***
c) Teaching leadership training or courses	97.9%	78.8%	19.1***

Note: ***indicates a difference at 0.001 significant level.

TALIS composites a principal leadership training index (PLEADERI) with different responses (never, prior to, after and both prior to and after serving as a principal) received on whether or not a principal has received the above three categories of education. "0" represents having received none, "1" represents little education,"2" represents a moderate level, and "3" represents a strong level of education. 97.6% of the lower secondary school principals indicate a strong education background while that of Singapore is 89.2% and the international average is 68.8%.

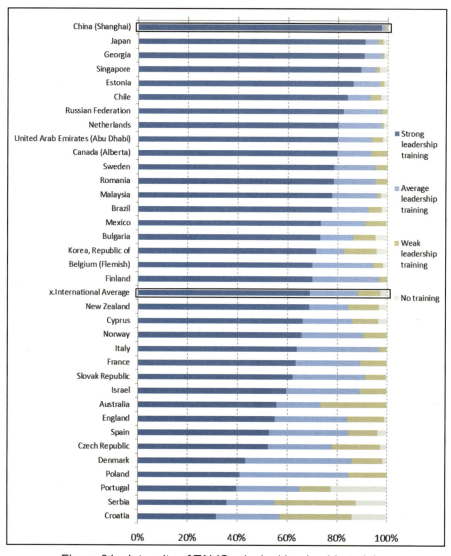

Figure 31   Intensity of TALIS principal leadership training

II. Professional development of principals

TALIS 2013 categorizes the professional development of teachers and principals into two groups, i.e. external and internal, and has examined the participation rate and intensity (participation during the past 12 months by days). The external professional development activities refer to courses, conferences or observation visits while the internal professional development activities refer to workshops, mentoring or research activities.

1. External professional development activities

94.9% of lower secondary school principals in Shanghai report participation in external professional development activities in the latest 12 months, which represents the second highest participation rate amongst all 36 TALIS 2013 (including TALIS 2013+) countries (regions) only after Singapore (99.3%). The TALIS average rests at 83.3% for this indicator. In terms of the duration, Shanghai takes the most advantageous edge in this regard with 94.9% of the principals stating they have spent 39.5 days in participating in the external professional development activities in the past 12 months, being in the first place across all TALIS 2013 (including TALIS 2013+) countries (regions). The international average suggests 13.6 days while Singapore reports 13.4 days by this indicator.

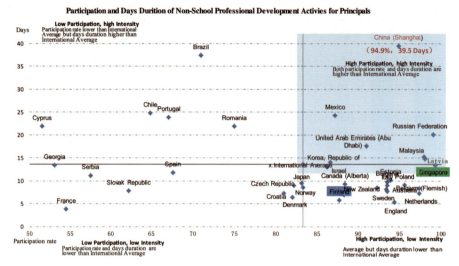

Figure 32   Participation and intensity of external professional
development (courses, conferences or observations)

2. Internal professional development activities

92.4% of lower secondary school principals in Shanghai report
participation in internal professional development activities in the
past 12 months, which represents the second highest participation
rate amongst all 36 TALIS 2013 (including TALIS 2013+) countries
(regions) only after Singapore (92.5%), while the TALIS average
is 52.6%. When it comes to the duration, Shanghai takes the most
advantageous edge in this regard with 92.4% of the principals stating
they have spent 39.1 days in participating in the internal professional
development activities in the past 12 months, being in the first place
across all TALIS 2013 (including TALIS 2013+) countries (regions).
The international average suggests 20.7 days while Singapore reports

15.5 days by this indicator.

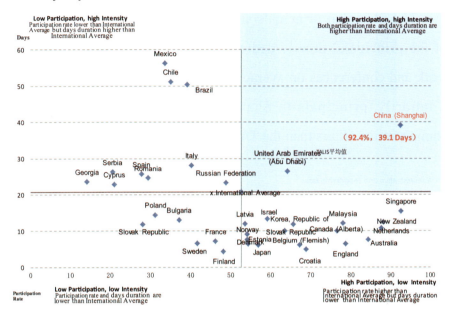

Figure 33   Participation and intensity of internal professional
development (workshops and mentoring)

III. Principals' work

1. Schedule of principals' routine work

Lower secondary school principals in Shanghai shoulder the responsibilities of teaching and administration at the same time. TALIS has examined the principals' average time allocation on routine work during an academic year and has come out with the results that a significant portion of time is spent on curriculum- or teaching-related work, ranking the first in this regard among all TALIS participating countries (regions).

The Shanghai principals survey results also indicate that 33% of the principals' time is dedicated to course- or teaching-related work and conferences on average while the TALIS average is 21.8%. Contrarily, principals in Shanghai spend less time (34.9%) on administrative affairs than the TALIS international average (41.5%).

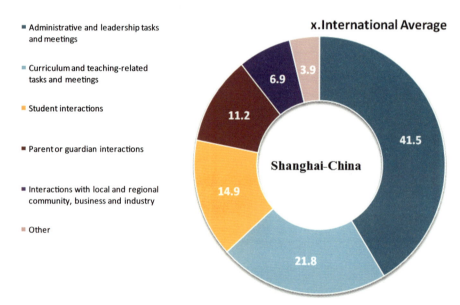

- Administrative and leadership tasks and meetings
- Curriculum and teaching-related tasks and meetings
- Student interactions
- Parent or guardian interactions
- Interactions with local and regional community, business and industry
- Other

Figure 34   Work time allocation of principals (%)

This reflects the principals in Shanghai are also teaching experts rather than administrators just focusing on administration and management to some extent, which is related to the sufficient pedagogical leadership trainings or courses received during principals' preparation education. In addition, results from TALIS also suggest a relatively weak connection between the lower secondary school principals in Shanghai with the outside world. Only 7.9% of principals' time is spent on interacting with parents or guardians, remarkably lower than TALIS average (11.2%). When it comes to interactions with the outside world such as communities and business premises, the proportion is only 5.6%, also significantly lower than TALIS average (6.9%). This indicates that principals in Shanghai need to further enhance their leadership influence.

2. Principals' frequently engaged work

TALIS also asked questions on what are the work that principals are frequently engaged in during the past 12 months, and the statistics reveal that promoting the collaboration between teaching and teachers is the keenest thing of principals.

91.1% of secondary school principals in Shanghai report "often" or "very often" for the question on whether they go to observe teaching in classes in the past 12 months while the TALIS average is only 52.3%. Nearly 90% of Shanghai principals say they "often" or "very often" support collaborations between teachers in action, so as to make sure that teachers do improve their pedagogical skills and are responsible for students' learning outcomes.

TALIS has consolidated a principals' instructional leadership index (PINSLEADS) for the answers to the above three questions. This index has a standard deviation of 2 with an intermediate point sets at 10. The PINSLEADS for lower secondary school principals in Shanghai is 12.1, significantly higher than the international average of 11.1. With no much difference to that of Singapore, Shanghai ranks 4th out of the 36 participating countries (regions) of TALIS.These figures characterize that the instructional leadership of principals in Shanghai centers on providing professional guidance and promoting teachers' professional development.

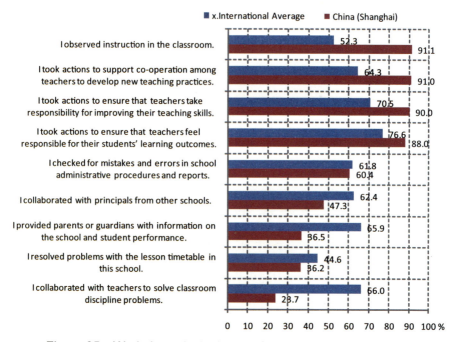

Figure 35   Work that principals are often or very often engaged
in the 12 months prior to this survey

Chapter Four: Discussions on TALIS Shanghai Results

I. Superiorities revealed by Shanghai survey results

1. A "trinity" of teachers policy

Since the reform and opening up, the professional development of basic education Shanghai teachers has gradually formed a Trinity mechanism which integrates three components including the promotion system of technical titles, appraisal system, and in-service training system. These inter-propelling systems not only motivate the professional development of teachers from within, but also provide strong support and incentives externally, boosting the continuous development of teachers' professional competency and in return plays a pivotal role in improving basic education in Shanghai.

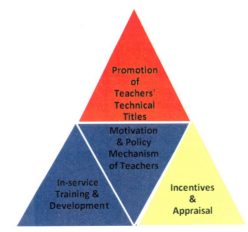

Figure 36　A "trinity" of Shanghai teachers policy

Statistics from TALIS suggest that the broadness and intensity of participation in professional development activities of Shanghai teachers go far beyond their counterparts in other countries and regions. Besides, Shanghai teachers contribute a participation rate higher than the international average in almost every professional development subject. All these evidence the powerful role that Shanghai's policy mechanism plays in teachers' professional development.

Though most of the countries attach great importance to the professional development of teachers, there are few countries that actually enjoy the synergy of the three, i.e. promotion system of teachers' technical titles, teachers' appraisal, and in-service development system. In many countries, teachers of basic education do not have promotion system of technical titles. Or in most cases, the promotion of technical titles mainly considers his/her length of teaching experience. Moreover, most countries lack clear requirements on teachers' in-service training and development, nor do they have an effective appraisal mechanism. This leads to the situation that, to a great extent, the in-service development for teachers relies on their self-consciousness of professionalism. However, the self-consciousness can not guarantee all teachers' participation in in-service professional development programmes. In particular, with the aging of the teachers and the emergence of career-tiredness, they will experience a sliding interest in in-service professional development. In that case, even if the government does offer various professional development programmes, the programmes can hardly function. Worse still, in some countries, in event of educational issues, teachers are the scapegoat to blame, or things go to the other extreme whereby the teachers are paid based on results.

Not only can the Shanghai Policy Trinity mobilize teachers' professional self-consciousness, but also provide the teachers with adequate support and supervision of professional development. Moreover, the Trinity strives to give positive feedback, ensuring the majority of the teachers embrace continuous progress and reducing their career-tiredness.

2. Teaching and researching policies anchoring in the schools, teachers, and teaching

The professional development activities of schools in Shanghai or even the entire China have become the most distinctive feature of teachers' development of basic education in China. The OECD special report for Shanghai points out that "compared with other TALIS countries (regions), Shanghai teachers enjoy a higher frequency in terms of participating in in-depth professional development activities". In particular, Shanghai teachers' participation rate of class observation and collaborative professional courses far exceeds the international average.

The extraordinary performance in in-depth professional development activities by Shanghai teachers is inevitably related to the teaching and researching policy that we hold for a long time. This policy dates back to 1950s, and till today, it has evolved to a comprehensive cohort embodying government bodies, professional research institutes, schools, and in-house teaching and researching teams. This also has become a key mechanism through which critical reforms on education are implemented. Data from TALIS show that three quarters of the Shanghai teachers report the teaching and researching teams and class preparation teams meet at least once every two weeks. Within the teaching and researching category, more than half of the participants report that the most frequent activities they attend are class observation and feedback as well as group preparation of teaching classes. Furthermore, approximately 90% of the teachers think that the research subjects mainly come from issues encountered in teaching practice. They also believe that research activities are helpful for improving teaching quality and summarizing teachers' knowledge of teaching practices.

Regardless of the teaching activities or researching activities, the most prominent characteristics are anchoring in schools, teachers, and teaching practices and venues. In other words, these activities are all school-oriented. Schools' teaching and researching policy provides a platform for exchanging information, sharing experience, sparkling ideas, and communicating feelings, becoming the most important forms of professional development for Shanghai teachers. Experts and teachers from various countries regard the "Teaching and Research Group", "Class Preparation Group", and "Grade Group" in Shanghai schools as "the most effective learning community for teachers".

3. Teachers' professional development is strongly supported by government and schools

It's for sure that teacher's professional development is important, yet not all countries and schools grant full support to teachers' professional development. On one hand, teachers' professional development requires investment of time, which will inevitably affect the arrangement of teachers' working time. In this regard, a relatively fewer hours of teaching workload lays a good foundation for Shanghai teachers to take part in the professional development activities, guaranteeing that teachers have enough time to participate in individual and group activities for professional development. At the same time, the Municipal Education Commission of Shanghai has sets a professional development baseline for teachers in different career phases, for example, 120 course hours for intern teachers, 360 course hours for teachers with no more than 5 years of work experience, and 540 course hours for senior teachers. The principals of lower secondary schools in Shanghai also attach great importance to professional development. 93% of lower secondary school principals make plans of professional development for the schools they are serving, which ensures the implementation of policies at the school-level. Results from TALIS also suggest that around 90% of Shanghai teachers believe that they have allocated fixed time within their working hours to participate in professional development activities, far beyond the international average.

On the other hand, teachers' professional development calls for a large amount of financial investment. Shanghai government keeps expanding its investment on teachers' training programmes, and has made it clear in the regulations that the municipal- and district-level governments need to make sure sufficient fund is devoted to teachers' training. Moreover, in the twelfth five-year plan period, schools are required to dedicate 100 RMB per student to teachers' training. Apart from the support of teachers' training programmes required by the governments and schools, governments also provides subsidies to teachers who pursue further in-service academic degree programmes. These measures strongly protect teachers' rights of enjoying professional development. Statistics from TALIS show that 80% of lower secondary school teachers in Shanghai do not need to pay for their professional development fees by themselves, significantly superior than most of other countries (regions).

Hence, from either the perspective of time or fund, Shanghai teachers receive great support in professional development. Nevertheless, approximately 60% of the teachers still point out that the conflict between the training time and work time remains the barrier for them to participate in professional development, and more than 50% of the teachers believe there is a lack of incentives to motivate teachers to take part in professional development. Therefore, support to teachers' professional development still needs more considerate time arrangement and precise incentive schemes.

4. Continue adopting new philosophies and methodologies with an open mind

As China's very first city to open up to the outside, Shanghai has already formed a convergence of multiple cultures. This great openness and tolerance are also manifested in the Shanghai's educational development featuring a spirit of learning, boldness, and innovation. Through continuous international exchanges and cooperation, education in Shanghai continues to adopt most updated philosophies and methodologies while innovating and evolving educational philosophies that are distinctive to Shanghai with combined considerations of its features and the reality. For example, the "Happy Education" and "Success Education" developed in early years and "Post-teahouse Education", "New Quality Schools", and "Green Indicators for Academic Quality" in recent years.

TALIS 2013 also shows a clear reflection of this characteristic. More than 90% of the teachers embrace the constructivist education philosophy and the ratio of teachers who agree that "thinking and reasoning are more important than specific course content" and "teachers shall give students opportunities to think prior to simply presenting solutions to them" is the highest among all participating countries (regions). Moreover, PISA results suggest that memorizing learning strategy is less using by Shanghai students than their counterparts in OECD while they use elaboration strategy more. This is obviously related to the characteristics of their teachers' educational philosophy.

5. Principals possess strong pedagogical leadership

A famous Chinese Educationist, TAO Xingzhi, once said, "a good principal means a good school." Teaching is the top priority for a school. Therefore, the importance of the pedagogical leadership of a principal to a school is evident.

TALIS data reveals that almost all principals (99.6%) have gone through principals' leadership trainings while only a mere 2% report that the formal education they received does not include pedagogical leadership training. This means more sufficient preparation in pedagogical leadership for principals in Shanghai compared with other countries and regions. Besides, principals in Shanghai also witness one of the highest participation rates and duration in both internal and external professional development activities, which guarantees the continuous attention paid to the pedagogical leadership competency by the principals themselves, and causes the principals attach greater importance, devote more time and energy to the pedagogical activities in schools.

Statistics from TALIS also demonstrate this characteristic of principals in Shanghai. Lower secondary school principals in Shanghai spend an average of 33% of their working time on course and teaching, 11 percentage points higher than TALIS average. Administration-wise, it is 6 percentage points lower than the TALIS average.This reflects that the principals in Shanghai place more emphasis on teaching out of their many responsibilities when compared with their counterparts from other countries.

II. Implications of Shanghai survey results

1. Pay attention to teachers' and principals' job satisfaction; improve work environment and enhancing teachers' recognition of their job

TALIS results indicate that Shanghai teachers are the least satisfied respondents with their profession, current working environment

71

and the overall job satisfaction rate is also the lowest, though a majority of the teachers (86.9%) do make a general comment of satisfaction of their work. In addition, though most of the principals agree that teacher as a profession is well respected in the society, they have low recognition of their professional status as a principal. Moreover, 97.5% of the principals in lower secondary school are generally satisfied with their work, but the satisfaction rate remains relatively low. This reminds us that more attention should be paid to these aspects.

Statistics from TALIS also show that teachers' job satisfaction significantly affect their work efficacy. Though satisfaction is a subjective feeling, it can definitely influence teacher's teaching practices. Hence, how to further improve the social status of primary and secondary school teachers, increasing teachers' total revenue and performance-related income, enhancing the work environment and building a team of proactive, passionate, caring and professional teachers remain an urgent problem to be resolved for Shanghai government.

2. Pay attention to teachers' professional development needs that are relevant to students' diversity

With the rising demand of the quality education, a more diverse mix of students, especially the educational pursuit of "education for the well-rounded development of every student", Shanghai teachers shall pay more attention to the diverse needs of students. TALIS discovers that teachers in Shanghai have already demonstrated much attention to the professional development activities in traditional teaching and learning areas. Yet in the field of teaching in multicultural or multilingual settings, teaching for students with special needs, and students' career guiding, the professional development activities remain few and need improvement. Currently, teaching in multicultural and multilingual setting reaches a limited group of audience, while the children of migrant workers require our keen considerations. Therefore, professional development programmes specifically designed for this group of students shall be in place.

Shanghai is undergoing reforms in its college entrance exam and admissions, shifting from emphasizing "scores only" to catering to students' individual strengths and future career plans when choosing the colleges or universities. This, from a certain perspective, forces the teachers to pay attention to students' personal development, learn to understand and identify students' personalities, foster students' interests and potentials, care about students' growth in different phases and offer assistance and guidance effectively.

3. Enhance the application of ICT and new technologies in teaching venues

With a growing emphasis on Information and Communication

Technology in teaching in recent years, there are more and more training activities in this regard. 63.9% of Shanghai teachers report participation in ICT-relevant professional development activities during the last 12 months while the percentage of teachers who need the training reaches 67.2%, both exceeding TALIS average. Yet, only 15% of the teachers in Shanghai ask the students to use ICT for project or homework, the percentage is only half of that in Singapore and 22.8 percentage points lower than the TALIS international average.

Besides, the TALIS average suggests that teaching-related ICT and new technologies in teaching are the top two areas amongst various professional development needs, reaching 59.5% and 56.1% respectively. Though teachers requiring professional development in these two areas take up 67.2% and 44.3% in Shanghai, the percentages are still small comparing with the other kinds of professional development needs.

Though the application of ICT and new technologies differs significantly in different countries (regions), and no evidence is identified suggesting that the more applications of ICT the better performance students get, there is a surging demand and reliance on using ICT and big data in students' future learning, working and living. This is inevitable since the information technology and new technologies are changing people's way of working and living and students are becoming "indigenous" of the era of ICT and big data.

4. Consider adjusting the assisting personnel ratio

In the lower secondary schools where the principals serve, there is an obvious shortage of assisting personnel. In particular, the number of teaching aids is remarkably smaller than other PISA high achievers such as Singapore, Finland, and Japan. Moreover, the teaching aids shortage is blocking the offering of quality education and a prominent factor affecting the job satisfaction of principals.

The student-teacher ratio in lower secondary schools in Shanghai is 11.3, significantly higher than international average (12.3). Compared with international average, schools in Shanghai are understaffed with of management assistants and teaching aids in particular. The teacher-management assistant ratio in lower secondary schools in Shanghai is 11.0 and the international average is 6.3, 8.2 and 2.7 for Finland and Singapore respectively. In other words, in the secondary schools in Shanghai, 1 management assistant support 11 teachers on average. Worse still, the ratio of teachers to teaching aids is 21.6 while the international average is 14.7, Singapore average is 11.9 and Finland average is 12.4. This number indicates that in the lower secondary schools in Shanghai, one teaching aid support 22 teachers on average, almost doubling the work load of a management assistant. Looking at PISA high scorers such as Singapore, Japan, Korea, Finland and Netherland, the averages for the above mentioned two indicators are both lower than the international average and

Shanghai average. This reveals that in the above listed countries, the staffing of assisting personnel is better than that in Shanghai.

Notably, when the age, gender, and education attainment factors are non-variables, the regression analysis of principals' job satisfaction against the shortage of school resources discovers a clear negative correlation between the principals' job satisfaction and teaching-related issues caused by the understaff of assisting personnel. This suggest that resolving the understaff issues is helpful for improving principals' job satisfaction.

5. Lower the entry criteria of principals' professional development activities, and enhancing principals' interactions with the society

The entry criteria for principals to participate in professional development is too high, which is not helpful for encouraging every principal to take part in their professional development activities. The top three reasons restricting lower secondary school principals' participation in professional development activities are "conflicting with work time" (26.2%), "not eligible" (12.5%), and "no incentives" (10.9%). When comparing with international average, we can see a relatively high proportion of principals in Shanghai believe that they "are not eligible" for attending the professional development activities, and the percentage is higher than all other TALIS 2013 participating countries or regions.

On average, principals in Shanghai spend less time interacting with students, parents and the outside world. TALIS 2013 has examined the work time allocation of principals throughout one academic year. The results show that Shanghai principals spend 14.1% of their working time interacting with students, 7.9% of the time interacting with parents, and 5.6% with the outside communities, which are all below international average. This reflects a relatively weak connection between the principals and the society and the community, indicating a weak sense of getting active educational resources and support from the outside world. Principals need to build up their capacity in this regard and enable every school to embrace better development with the understanding and support from all walks of life.

Afterword

"Teacher And Learning International Survey"(TALIS) is another large-scale international research programme on educational evaluation that Shanghai participates in after the "Programme of International Student Assessment" (PISA). Upon the closing of this cycle of research, our team would like to express our greatest gratitude to all people who have worked hard to the research. It is the vision and funding of the Shanghai Municipal Education Commission, the support from various departments including Human Resources, Foreign Affairs, Finance and Basic Education Department, the thorough understanding of our research programme from Shanghai Normal University, the cohesive institutional collaboration from district- or county-level education bureaus, admission offices, and information offices, and the patience and timely responses from 200 sampling schools and over 4000 teachers and principals that made such a large-scale, high-standard international survey executed. Amazingly, the eye-catching results drawn from this international lower secondary school teachers survey in Shanghai collectively reflect the accomplishments attained in building the team of teachers by the city during the past three decades of reform and opening up. Moreover, the results demonstrate the teachers' passion for career, enthusiasm for life, and pursuit of perfection and life-long development. The research team pays greater awe to primary and secondary school teachers as well as our peer workers in Shanghai's education sector after collecting the research data.

This research project is chaired by Prof. ZHANG Minxuan, relying on the Research Institute for International and Comparative Education, SHNU to complete. The research report is also compiled under Prof. ZHANG's planning, editing, and confirmation. Credit goes to Dr. ZHU Xiaohu for compositing Chapter One, Two and Four and Dr. XU Jinjie for Chapter Three. Prof. ZHANG Minxuan reviewed and amended the entire book. Upon publication of this book, we would like to extend our appreciation to Shanghai Educational Press, especially to the editor Tongliang and Zhouji, without whom this report will never goes to the readers.

ZHANG Minxuan

10 March 2017

图书在版编目(CIP)数据

专业与卓越 : 2015年上海教师教学国际调查结果概要 : 汉英
对照 / 教师教学国际调查中国上海项目组著. —上海 : 上海
教育出版社,2017.6
ISBN 978-7-5444-7692-8

Ⅰ.①专... Ⅱ.①教... Ⅲ.①初中—中学教师—师资培
养—调查研究—上海—2015—汉、英 Ⅳ.①G635.12

中国版本图书馆CIP数据核字(2017)第161767号

责任编辑 童　亮
封面设计 周　吉

专业与卓越
——2015 年上海教师教学国际调查结果概要(汉英对照)
教师教学国际调查中国上海项目组　著

出　　版　上海世纪出版股份有限公司
　　　　　上 海 教 育 出 版 社
　　官　网 www.seph.com.cn
　　易文网 www.ewen.co
地　　址　上海市永福路 123 号
邮　　编　200031
发　　行　上海世纪出版股份有限公司发行中心
印　　刷　上海书刊印刷有限公司
开　　本　700×1000　1/16　印张 9.25　插页 2
版　　次　2017 年 8 月第 1 版
印　　次　2017 年 8 月第 1 次印刷
书　　号　ISBN 978-7-5444-7692-8/G·6348
定　　价　60.00 元(全二册)

(如发现质量问题,读者可向工厂调换)